The Competent Pastor

The Competent Pastor

Skills and Self-Knowledge for Serving Well

Ronald D. Sisk

THE
ALBAN
INSTITUTE

Herndon, Virginia
www.alban.org

Cover design by Adele Robey, Phoenix Graphics.

Library of Congress Cataloging-in-Publication Data

Sisk, Ronald D.
    The competent pastor : skills and self-knowledge for serving well / Ronald D. Sisk.
        p.   cm.
    ISBN 1-56699-304-0
    1. Pastoral theology.   I. Title.

BV4011.3.S57 2005
253—dc22

2005024217

09   08   07   06   05   UG   1   2   3   4   5

Contents

Preface

This book is intended to help ministers, seminarians, and laypeople who work with ministers to understand two concepts:

1. What does it mean to say that a minister is *competent?*
2. How does a competent minister *function?*

Competence, briefly, we will define as the ability to do what needs to be done. Sometimes that means understanding yourself or others. Sometimes it means getting some task accomplished in the church. Always it means keeping a realistic perspective on your own life as a human being, a Christian, and a minister—what works for you and what doesn't.

A competent minister functions, then, by moving forward toward understanding, resolution, ministry, and self-fulfillment. She will be happy in her job or able to figure out why she's not happy, and will be capable of moving forward. He won't get stuck. Or, at least, when he does get stuck, he'll know some specific steps to take to get unstuck.

As professor of homiletics and Christian ministry at North American Baptist Seminary in Sioux Falls, South Dakota, I find that a good portion of my work focuses on making certain that our graduates take with them the necessary understanding and skills to function as ministers of the gospel. The book arises out of a self-assessment assignment which the seminary requires of seniors in its master of divinity program. The seniors are required to evaluate their understanding and skill in 10 specific areas. Those 10 areas, the last two combined, form the nine chapters of this book. I'm convinced that these areas constitute the basis for ministerial competence.

Acknowledgments

As a pastor for 20 years myself, I've brought to bear a good number of my own experiences, both joys and frustrations, in these pages. In addition, because no minister has an exclusive corner on competence, I've sought comments from three colleagues in ministry—a male pastor, a female pastor, and an expert in pastoral care. Their insights, which are printed as marginal notes, should add depth and texture which no work of this kind could attain coming from one person alone. I'm exceedingly grateful to James Hyde, Judie Mattison, and Mike Smith, whose initials appear at the end of their respective comments, for working this project into their busy schedules. Mike is a Baptist pastor in Tennessee. Judie is a Lutheran minister in Wisconsin. James serves in the pastoral care department of a Presbyterian seminary in Kentucky. From different life journeys and different theological perspectives, their contributions are invaluable.

I would especially like to thank my Alban Institute editor Beth Gaede for her encouragement, patience, and insight as the project has unfolded. Special thanks to copy editor Jean Caffey Lyles for her meticulous and good-humored work in shaping the final form of the manuscript. Thanks are also due to Dr. Benjamin Leslie, vice president and academic dean of North American Baptist Seminary, for giving me time and permission to write as part of my responsibilities. Thanks to the students of the spring 2004 Readiness for Ministry Colloquium, who generously allowed their self-assessments to become part of the basis for this project. Thanks to the congregations of the Forks of Elkhorn Baptist Church, Tiburon Baptist Church, Western Hills Baptist Church, and Crescent Hill Baptist Church, who put up with me as their pastor. Thanks to my wife, Sheryl, and son Doug, who make this minister's personal life a joy day by day. Most of all, of course, thanks be to God, who gives us the victory through our Lord Jesus Christ!

The Competent Pastor

ONE

From My Mother's Womb

Comprehending Where You Come From

Pastor Ed Franklin locked the church door and jogged wearily to his car. To add to his mood of misery, it was raining. Once behind the wheel, he couldn't find the energy to start the car. He just sat there damp and disgusted with himself. Nothing in his theology or ministerial training had taught him to be a doormat. But a doormat he seemed to be.

The meeting of the church board had started like a dozen others in recent months. Routine matters were dispensed with as quickly as possible, and the board turned its attention to the next step in the strategic plan. The church had been working on the plan for about six months now. After the usual introductory sermons, "town meetings," and congregational surveys, the committees had reported their recommendations to the board. Now it was the board's job to distill the mound of material into a coherent three- to five-year plan.

Like most pastors, Ed had been content to allow the process to work, believing that the congregation would surface the issues that needed to be addressed. He very much wanted them to take ownership of the process. There were just one or two points on which he held strong opinions about what needed to be done.

One of those was the church preschool. As an aging congregation with relatively few young families, the church had allowed the preschool area to become distinctly shabby in recent years. There were few toys. Carpets in the entire area were worn and dirty. During the last renovation a decade and a half ago, someone had decided that the proper color for children's areas was beige, and that lighting should be subdued. As a result, the entire area felt depressing and uninviting.

Ed believed strongly that the preschool area should be first in line for renovation. As the parent of a preschooler himself, he knew that young families would not be attracted to the current facility. What he hadn't counted on, however, was the strength of the worship lobby.

Susan Sparks led the charge. "We can't put the preschool first. The sanctuary hasn't been redone in 15 years. We need paint. We need carpet. We need screens. We need a new sound system and more light." She had a good argument, but Ed believed that his case for the preschool was stronger.

What surprised him was that he couldn't force himself to make the case. He sat there and let Susan carry the day. What was wrong with him? Why did he feel so guilty even when he knew he was right? Why was confrontation so hard? Susan hadn't worried about expressing her opinion. Why couldn't Ed bring himself to argue his?

Miserable, replaying the meeting again and again in his mind, Ed found his thoughts drifting back to his parents' fights when he was a child. How he had hated those fights! How he had wanted the shouting to stop! Why couldn't people just get along?

The Influence of Your Family of Origin

There's a lot of me in Pastor Ed. As the middle child of parents who were both adult children of alcoholics, I learned early on how important it was to keep the peace. What I never learned either in seminary or in my early years of ministry was how much those childhood patterns of behavior and coping strategies would affect my work as a pastor.

It's not that awareness of such an effect is particularly new. From the time of Edwin H. Friedman's pioneering work *Generation to Generation: Family Process in Church and Synagogue*,[1] the pastoral care community has known that the minister's own family system plays a significant role in the way he or she functions. Some works on leadership and pastoral practice—such as Reggie McNeal's *A Work of Heart: Understanding How God Shapes Spiritual Leaders*—have begun to include sections highlighting family-of-origin and current-family concerns.[2] (Note that for purposes of this chapter I shall refer to "family of origin" to mean both our birth family and our current family.) Unfortunately this basic insight has yet to find its way into the general curriculum in many seminaries. The counseling program of the seminary where I teach deals extensively with systems theory. Our introductory supervised ministry class uses McNeal's book as a text. Even here, though, classes in family systems are an elective and not a requirement for the ministerial degree. Across North America, the vast majority of master of divinity students can make it through their entire program without ever dealing seriously with the impact of their own family of origin on their personal and ministerial function.

We are, of course, intuitively aware that there is such an effect. At the seminary I attended, a number of the students were second- and third-generation ministers. As an electrician's son, I knew beyond doubt that many of my classmates had absorbed lessons on ministerial practice at the family table. Those of us from nonministerial or unchurched backgrounds complained regularly about our relative disability. We thought becoming good ministers was somehow a matter of "catching up."

I knew that I needed to learn to eat with the local business folk at the country club, to don the proper ministerial dress, and to know when to speak and when to keep silent. We didn't think nearly so much about the way all of us, whatever our background, carry our family dynamics with us into every situation we face.

I remember seeing an assigned counselor before starting seminary. She looked at my history as that of one who came from a dysfunctional family and the child who had to manage the family problems. She asked how I handled difficult, stressful times. I told her that I usually just put my head down and walked into the blizzard. "You'll have to find additional ways of coping when you're in ministry," she told me. "How will you take care of yourself? You won't have much to offer a congregation when you're exhausted." JM*

It's not difficult to understand why we ministers may tend to discount the influence of our family of origin. First, the Christian faith is about conversion, about new beginnings. Our ideology tells us that people can change. So we try to live as though we *have* changed. Ministers, particularly, are expected to reflect the image of Christ in our behavior. Augustine doesn't tell us about day-to-day

---

*The sidebar comments were written by three colleagues in ministry: Judie Mattison (JM), James A. Hyde (JAH), and Mike Smith (MS).

struggles with chastity *after* his conversion. Pastor Marie, who was sexually abused by her big, strong elder brother, shouldn't, we seem to believe, let that affect the way she deals with the big, strong farmers of her rural parish. Her Christian faith should help her rise above her pain. The faith is about *metanoia*, transformation, but we seem to forget that a transformation often needs to go much deeper than surface behaviors. For many of us, whole areas of behavior shaped by our past may need to be brought to awareness so that they can be transformed.

Edwin Friedman's theory is based on the family-systems work of Murray Bowen *(Family Theory in Clinical Practice* [New York: J. Aronson, 1978]). Bowen's work is widely used but has also been critiqued by Deborah Anna Luepnitz *(The Family Interpreted: Feminist Theory in Clinical Practice* [New York: Basic Books, 1988]). Luepnitz argues that the theory often leaves women out of key considerations and may overimplicate the mother in dysfunction while minimizing the father's role. Bowen also minimizes the importance of emotion. You may need to pay more attention to your own feelings and the feelings of your congregation as you think about the system. Ministers sometimes relate too much from a thinking rather than a feeling point of view. JAH

Second, as a result of discounting the power of our past, we have failed to deal adequately with the conjunction of emotional, behavioral, and spiritual factors in our personal ministerial development. For example, as the child of two adult children of alcoholics, I carry with me family behavior patterns and coping mechanisms which my parents learned during their own dysfunctional upbringings—avoiding conflict, holding in anger, taking responsibility for others' behavior. If I do not understand those patterns and their potential influence upon my own behavior, I am at risk of living out those patterns for another generation. I may stuff down my anger toward a church member who annoys me until, reaching the limit of my endurance, I explode. This risk is real *regardless of my spiritual commitment and sincere desire to follow Christ.* The fact that the church tends naïvely to assume that commitment to Christ obviates such risk means that we don't pay nearly enough attention to the psychological formation of our ministerial candidates.

Third, seminary curricula tend to focus on academic "content courses." These traditional, necessary, and demanding courses in languages, biblical interpretation, history, and theology provide students with a knowledge of what the church has done in the past. Field experience courses help students with the nuts and bolts of pastoral practice. Pastoral care classes provide a basic introduction to Christian psychology and care for members in crisis. Only rarely do these content courses provide a place in which the student is compelled to address his or her personal background and its role in ministerial function.

As a part of my preparation for writing this chapter, I read the self-assessments of a number of senior students in our school's final supervised ministry course. The course is designed to help students approaching graduation to synthesize what they have learned. We require them to address in their self-assessment the influence of their family of origin on their personal ministerial formation. They were as bright, committed, and mature a bunch of folk as any seminary is likely to boast. Yet, with the exception of a handful who had studied family systems, their observations in this section of their papers tended to be superficial and minimally reflective. "My happy childhood made me a good minister," or "My unhappy marriage makes me a good minister," simply isn't enough. If we don't understand the patterns of behavior a happy childhood or an unhappy marriage may generate, we are likely to repeat those patterns in our ministry.

The question, then, is "How do I develop an understanding of the possible influence of my family of origin upon my own behavior in ministry?" The rest of this chapter will seek to answer that question.

Note that there is a difference between the American Association of Pastoral Counselors and the American Association of Christian Counselors. Some professionals make a distinction between Christian counseling and pastoral counseling. For more information on this distinction, log on to www.aapc.org or www.aacc.net. JAH

An Approach: Understanding Family of Origin

Pastor Ed from our introductory vignette found himself unable to confront members, even though the matter under discussion was important to him. Clearly he was unhappy with his performance in the meeting. You could take an individualistic perspective and argue that Ed lacks fortitude or character. You could say that he's dysfunctional or, as he himself said, "a doormat." You could, of course, spiritualize Ed's problem and say, as many in evangelical circles might, that he hadn't prayed sufficiently about the meeting or that he failed to trust the Holy Spirit to guide his comments. Or you could take a psychoanalytical view and say that he's the victim of deep-seated personal insecurities stemming from his early experiences with dominant women. Each of these perspectives may have a certain validity. None of them, though, is likely either to give Ed any comfort or to help him perform more appropriately the next time he's in a similar situation. To use Friedman's language, Ed is "stuck."

Traditionally the church has tended to view self-defeating behaviors such as Ed's as evidence of our sinful human nature. With the apostle Paul, you and I and Ed "do not understand [our] own actions. For [we] do not do what [we] want, but [we] do the very thing [we] hate" (Rom. 7:15). The writer of Hebrews, pointing to the example of those who have gone before us in the faith, calls us beyond such limitations: "[L]et us also lay aside every weight and the sin that clings so closely, and let us run with perseverance the race that is set before us, looking to Jesus" (Heb. 12: 1b-2a). But the usual view in church tradition has been that these weights or sins can be conquered by repentance, force of character, prayer, and the power of the Holy Spirit.

The interesting point here is that even the Scriptures just cited seem to recognize the inadequacy of any simplistic solution to the problems that drag us down. Paul writes from the perspective of mature Christian commitment. Even as an apostle, he struggles to comprehend why he does what he does and why he can't seem to change behaviors he abhors. One might argue that in a sense the whole of Christian history has been a frustrating pilgrimage toward purity, as we seek the means by which believers can attain the spiritual and behavioral health into which Christ calls us.

The rise of the science of psychology and, in the latter half of the twentieth century, Christian psychology,[3] has provided a key interpretive framework in this search. Pastors come to ministry knowing that hidden reasons may account for why we and our parishioners behave the way we do. We come to pastoral practice also with some ideas about how to uncover and treat those root causes of behavior, or at least with a sense that we can refer ourselves or others to someone who can uncover and treat those causes. The benefits of pastoral counseling for parishioners are substantial—especially in regard to their becoming more self-aware and internalizing the experience of grace. Mental health has become recognized as a necessary factor in spiritual health.

Friedman's work adds another interpretive psychological lens, one that has specific application to healthy pastoral practice:

> A family approach to organized religious life touches upon major personal and practical issues in the professional life of the clergy. With regard to personal issues, it has relevance for the dilemmas of intimacy, expectations, privacy, being a model, or being oneself, refreshment, feeling of competence, adequacy, and isolation, etc. It can even be applied to crises in personal faith. The family approach can also be extended to preaching.
>
> Professionally . . . family systems theory offers new perspectives and approaches for clergy-congregational problems and the stress experienced by clergy at such times. In addition, because the family approach is based on an organic model, it offers a way of thinking about this . . . that is far less blaming and far less polarizing. A systems approach, as always, tends to redistribute the guilt and take the sting out of toxic issues.[4]

Friedman goes on to detail six basic family-systems concepts which he believes have particular application to understanding what goes in the church:

- *Homeostasis.* This phenomenon is "the tendency of any set of relationships to strive perpetually, in self-corrective ways, to preserve the organizing principles of its existence."[5] A system strives to maintain balance, to keep things the way they have been. When a pastor tries to change things, or experiences family problems, or when a church member experiences problems, the stress of change will throw the system out of balance. Any change in one part of a system inevitably affects the system as a whole, but systems resist that upset. *problem of systems*
- *Process and Content.* Content issues, the specific matter of complaints, are often red herrings for process issues. "Every time members of a congregation begin to concentrate on their

minister's *'performance,'* there's a good chance they are displacing something from their own personal lives."[6] Focusing on the content of complaints won't deal with the systemic issues and the nature of people's interactions.

- *Nonanxious Presence.* Ministers can often defuse conflict by refusing to diagnose a problem as somebody's particular issue and by remaining playful in the midst of tension. You don't say, "This church's problems would be over if Ethel Green would just leave." You do say, "If we don't figure out how to meet this budget, I'm going to have to go back to sermons by candlelight."

- *Overfunctioning.* When a minister takes on personal and exclusive responsibility for the well-being of the church, we say that he or she is "overfunctioning." Ministers who are overfunctioning manifest anxiety and create situations in which congregation members can ignore or deny their appropriate responsibility.

These must be avoided.... to Pastors oyt to train people against this in the middle of their formation.

- *Triangles.* Church life is full of triangled relationships. A triangle is created whenever anyone in the church wants you to get someone else in the church to do (or not to do) something. You become one corner of the triangle. People are always wanting to put the minister in the middle. That way, they don't have to take responsibility for what happens. The tragedy is that ministers often allow themselves to be put there. Learning to detriangulate situations can keep communication honest and direct.

- *Identified Patient.* Ministers often find themselves the "identified patient" in a church's problems. They take on too much responsibility for whatever goes wrong. When people in the church begin complaining, ministers often isolate themselves from the layleaders, who tend to be both intensely interdependent and unable "to take well-defined positions independent of the complainers."[7] The minister falls under stress and tends to become dysfunctional. Everybody decides it's the minister's fault, except the minister, who tends to blame the complainers. In fact, it's the system.

Developing an understanding of these concepts and their roots in systems theory provides a kind of template that a minister can use to gain perspective on the dynamics of church relationships. In other words, Ed can be offered a new lens for viewing his behavior at the meeting, a lens that may clarify his view in at least three directions.

First, it may help him understand the family system in which he grew up. Since Ed's parents were the children of alcoholics, they may have been part of a family system in which one or both of them functioned as "enablers," working to maintain the family equilibrium, or homeostasis, while their parents misbehaved. Ed may have in turn taken over that role, becoming the designated peacemaker in his own family. If so, he may have grown up seeing confrontation as taboo for him. To fight for what he believes would be to abandon his role as peacemaker, and that would be difficult indeed for him. Ed is most likely overfunctioning.

A second lens Ed could use would be to look at his role in his present family. Ed may still function as peacemaker for his parents, even though he no longer lives in the same house. He may also, because he was raised in the role of peacemaker, find it difficult to confront problems healthily within his marriage. In Jane Austen's novel *Pride and Prejudice*, Mr. Bennet diagnoses his elder daughter's chances for a happy marriage by saying that she and her fiancé are "both so amiable that nothing will ever be resolved." Ed could be living out some such scenario in his own domestic life.

Understanding his role in his family of origin, both past and present, is a vital part of Ed's understanding how he responds in his professional life. He may realize, for example, that he's taking far too much emotional responsibility for avoiding conflict in the church board meeting. He is overfunctioning in his relationship to the church. Who ever said it's a pastor's responsibility to keep peace in the church at all costs? Did not Jesus himself frequently confront others, even when he knew they would not welcome what he had to say?

Will understanding the role of his family of origin in shaping his behavior make Ed a virtuoso at confrontation? Probably not. In discussing another pastoral example on a voyage of self-discovery, McNeal observes cogently, "Richard will always be vulnerable at these points. He will always walk with a limp. Like Jacob after his encounter with the angel at Jabbock, Richard will have the limp as a trophy of his wrestling with God. . . . All leaders limp. Leaders become leaders, in part, because they are willing to wrestle with who

McNeal   *Work & Har* @ 117

they are, who they want to become, how they can overcome some deficit in their own lives."[8] Realizing that he works from perspectives he learned in his family of origin won't solve all of Ed's problems. Neither will it solve yours or mine. But it will help us to see more clearly what we are doing. And that will help us move toward doing something about it.

Finally, Ed could gain by turning the family-systems lens in one other direction, toward the church as a whole. Churches operate as family systems. Friedman says:

> Of all work systems, however, the one that functions most like a family is the church or synagogue. This is true in part because it is so difficult for clergy to distinguish home life from professional life (whether or not there is a parsonage and whether or not the spouse is deeply invested), and partly because the intensity with which some lay people become invested in their religious institutions makes the church or synagogue a prime arena for the displacement of important unresolved family issues."[9]

So... we probably shouldn't complicate things with unnecessary systems!

In other words, the church operates as both a family system in itself and as an interlocking system of systems comprising the families from which both clergy and laity spring. How people act at church is inevitably affected by what's going on at home. It's essential to understand the relationships within and among your church's families if you want to understand why members act the way they act.

In a similar vein, Lloyd Rediger's insightful book *Clergy Killers: Guidance for Pastors and Congregations Under Attack*[10] observes that some congregations may develop systems that are toxic for generations, destroying pastor after pastor precisely to keep the church itself from having to change. Note that no one is attacking Ed, at least as far as Ed knows. If Ed presses his case for change, however, it's more than possible that someone will. Such attacks often come not from personal animosity or because of mental illness as such, but from an unrecognized compulsion to protect the homeostasis of the system.

Viewing the entire congregation through a family-systems lens might also help Ed understand his antagonist, Susan. Susan's role in the church family system, and likely in her own family of origin, may help explain aspects of the role she took in that meeting of the church board. Let's say, for example, that Susan is a third-generation member of the church. Her grandparents helped found the congregation as a bastion of traditional, formal worship against the winds of revivalism sweeping the denomination in the 1950s. Without necessarily realizing it herself, she has become the guardian of tradition, the guarantor of homeostasis. She believes that worship should be primary in the church's priorities, and even the prospect of new families makes her uneasy that the church might change. By realizing how these factors may be at work in Susan's position, Ed can both defuse any personal antagonism he may feel toward Susan and search for ways to enlist her as an ally rather than an opponent. In addition, if he understands the way his own family-of-origin issues play into his behavior, he may be able to learn both to stand his ground in confrontations and to avoid the typical overreaction of being provoked into hostilities with Susan. He may also be able to keep himself from getting triangulated in the relationship between the worship traditionalists and the children's advocates in the church. He could, for example, suggest a meeting of the two groups to search for common ground.

In discussing a difficult change process in the synagogue of which he was rabbi for a number of years, Friedman discusses how dissent over a congregation's direction can lead to polarization and distance between the minister and those with whom he or she disagrees. Congregations, by and large, hate change and work hard to maintain homeostasis, even when the status quo is no longer working.[11] In his congregation Friedman dealt with dissent not by changing his position but by increasing his nonanxious, listening conversation with the congregation as a whole, especially with his opposition, [12] and by injecting an element of playfulness into a tense situation.

A family-systems approach to the minister's personal and professional life is both more complex and considerably more detailed than I've been able to show in these brief pages. What I hope this overview achieves, however, is to provide at least a hint of the kind of benefit a minister can derive from understanding how our own families and our congregations operate as relationship systems.

Assessing Your Church and Family System

A systems approach to thinking about families and churches is obviously new for many of us. If you're drawn to the idea, though, you may want to begin thinking about your own family system and your church's family system. The following ideas gleaned from the literature are designed to help you do just that. The brief book list at the end of the chapter should take you well down the road toward understanding this dynamic approach.

Family Structure and Function

All families have structure, and all families function. But the structure of a family does not necessarily reveal how it functions. In his book *How Your Church Family Works*, Peter L. Steinke, a Lutheran pastor and former director of clergy care for Lutheran Social Services, provides a comparison of the structure and function of a well known biblical family.[13]

Obviously the patriarchal family charted on page 15 didn't function as it was structured. Neither does yours or mine. Try imitating Steinke's diagram for three generations of your own family of origin. What is its structure? What functional lines can you draw? Note that Steinke draws a single line to indicate an emotional connection, a double line to indicate emotional fusion, and a dotted line to indicate a broken relationship. Who in your own family seems more connected than is healthy? What emotional barriers exist? What does this tell you about your way of functioning within and outside the family?

Family History

Another way of assessing your family's functioning is to do an abbreviated family history. On a piece of paper make four columns. Label the first column "Timeline." Begin with your parents' date of marriage, or with your birth if no marriage took place. Label the second column "Milestones." Mark major positive events in your family's life; for example, the birth of a child, the purchase of a new house. Label the third column "Endings." Include deaths, divorces, loss of job, and so forth. Label the fourth column "Stressors." List any event, positive or negative, that doesn't belong in column two or three. If divorce and remarriage take place, indicate that and follow the line of the new primary relationship. If you're single, include

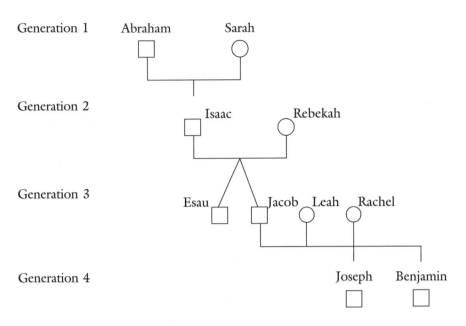

1. Family Structure

Generation 1 — Abraham — Sarah

Generation 2 — Isaac — Rebekah

Generation 3 — Esau — Jacob — Leah — Rachel

Generation 4 — Joseph — Benjamin

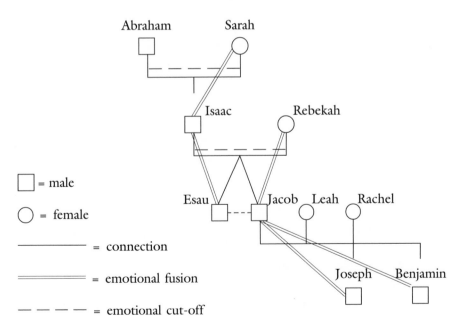

2. Family Functioning

Abraham — Sarah

Isaac — Rebekah

Esau — Jacob — Leah — Rachel

Joseph — Benjamin

□ = male

○ = female

——— = connection

═══ = emotional fusion

— — — = emotional cut-off

Adapted from *How Our Church Family Works: Understanding Congregations as Emotional Systems,* by Peter L. Steinke (Alban Institute, 1993), page 35. Used by permission.

events from your parents' lives and from your own. See the sample below from my own family history. Note that most milestones could also be stressors.

Timeline	Milestones	Endings	Stressors
May 9, 1941	Dorothy Richards and Ray Sisk marry		
Dec. 7, 1941			Pearl Harbor Attack
Early 1942	Ray enters Navy		Dorothy moves to Indianapolis
Sept. 2, 1942	Ann born		
Fall 1943	Ray gets leave		
July 15, 1944	Teddy Ray born		
August 1945		War ends	

If you have made a chart of your own, what do you learn from this overview of your family's history about your family members' strategies for making decisions? Coping with change? Grieving losses? Celebrating? What do you learn about your own strategies in these arenas?

Now do the same thing for your church's history. Begin with its founding. If your church is more than 100 years old, go back to a watershed event within the memory of your oldest member. Label the four columns "Timeline," "Additions," "Losses," and "Stressors." What patterns emerge in your church's family history?

Family Health

Another way of assessing the health of your family of origin comes from a simple scale developed by the American Association for Marriage and Family Therapy. This scale applies to the family in which you grew up. Obviously this instrument is not a final indicator of the health of your family system. It can be used, however, to begin the process of thinking about your family's competence in coping with the stresses of life.

Rate the following 40 items, for your family of origin as you remember it. Use the following scale and circle the appropriate number:

5 Strongly agree that it describes my family of origin
4 Agree that it describes my family of origin
3 Neutral
2 Disagree that it describes my family of origin
1 Strongly disagree that it describes my family of origin

1. It was normal to show both positive and negative feelings.   5 4 3 2 1

2. The atmosphere was usually unpleasant.   5 4 3 2 1

3. We encouraged one another to develop new friendships.   5 4 3 2 1

4. Differences of opinion were discouraged.   5 4 3 2 1

5. People often made excuses for their mistakes.   5 4 3 2 1

6. My parents encouraged family members to listen to one another.   5 4 3 2 1

7. Conflicts never got resolved.   5 4 3 2 1

8. My family taught me that people were basically good.   5 4 3 2 1

9. I found it difficult to understand what other family members said and how they felt.   5 4 3 2 1

10. We talked about our sadness when a relative or family friend died.   5 4 3 2 1

11. My parents openly admitted it when they were wrong.   5 4 3 2 1

12. I expressed just about any feeling I had.   5 4 3 2 1

13. Resolving conflicts was a very stressful experience.   5 4 3 2 1

14. My family was receptive to the different ways various family members viewed life.   5 4 3 2 1

15. My parents encouraged me to express my views openly.   5 4 3 2 1

16. I often had to guess at what other family members thought or how they felt.   5 4 3 2 1

17. My attitudes and my feelings frequently were ignored or criticized.   5 4 3 2 1

18. My family members rarely expressed responsibility for their actions.   5 4 3 2 1

19. I felt free to express my own opinions.   5 4 3 2 1
20. We never talked about our grief when a   5 4 3 2 1
    relative or family friend died.
21. Sometimes in my family, I did not have to   5 4 3 2 1
    say anything but I felt understood.
22. The atmosphere was cold and negative.   5 4 3 2 1
23. The members of my family were not very   5 4 3 2 1
    receptive to one another's views.
24. I found it easy to understand what other   5 4 3 2 1
    family members said and how they felt.
25. If a family friend moved away, we never   5 4 3 2 1
    discussed our feelings of sadness.
26. I learned to be suspicious of others.   5 4 3 2 1
27. I felt that I could talk things out and settle   5 4 3 2 1
    conflicts.
28. I found it difficult to express my own opinions.   5 4 3 2 1
29. Mealtimes in my home usually were friendly   5 4 3 2 1
    and pleasant.
30. No one cared about the feelings of other   5 4 3 2 1
    family members.
31. We usually were able to work out conflicts.   5 4 3 2 1
32. Certain feelings were not allowed to be expressed.   5 4 3 2 1
33. My family believed that people usually   5 4 3 2 1
    took advantage of you.
34. I found it easy to express what I thought and   5 4 3 2 1
    how I felt.
35. My family members usually were sensitive   5 4 3 2 1
    to one another's feelings.
36. When someone important to us moved   5 4 3 2 1
    away, our family discussed our feelings of loss.
37. My parents discouraged us from expressing   5 4 3 2 1
    views different from theirs.
38. People took responsibility for what they did.   5 4 3 2 1
39. My family had an unwritten rule: Don't   5 4 3 2 1
    express your feelings.
40. I remember my family as being warm and   5 4 3 2 1
    supportive.

The closer to 200 your total score, the better your family's health.[14]

Triangles

One more key assessment idea should help you begin to apply systems thinking to your relationship with your church (and perhaps with your own family). Let's draw some triangles! In the case study, Pastor Ed felt triangled between the worship advocates and the children's advocates in his church. Each was pulling him in a different direction. Draw that triangle on a piece of paper. How might Ed "detriangulate" that situation? The answer is fairly simple. Ed needs the line between the worship people and the children's advocates to become a line of communication rather than one of conflict. In the church board meeting he might have answered Susan: "Your perspective is a good one, Susan, but our children's leaders are seeing the situation differently." He could then have turned to the children's leader in the room and asked for that perspective.

Take a moment to think about triangles in your family of origin. Did your mother ever want you to help get your father or brother or sister or grandparent to do something? Did people talk directly *with* each other or talk *about* each other with others in the family? How do you communicate in your current family? Do you ever try to triangulate family members? Can you see relationship triangles in your church? Whenever a church member wants you to get another member to do something, a bell (or a triangle!) should ring in your head.

In my experience, we need a daily or at least a repetitive routine that encourages us to apply the kinds of insights discussed here. For example, I keep an informal journal. Over the past two decades, I've made a point of posing a particular question to myself in my journal entries: "Is there something in my family background, a church member's family background, or the larger family structure of my congregation driving the situation in question?" I find that the answers often help me discover a better way to deal with the current situation. Reading through the accumulated journal entries also enables me to develop and refine my understanding of my congregation's family systems. MAS

Further Reading

If you'd like to understand more about the systems approach to church and family life, I recommend the following books, used in the preparation of this chapter:

Friedman, Edwin H. *Generation to Generation: Family Process in Church and Synagogue.* New York: Guilford Press, 1985.

Lewis, Jerry M. *How's Your Family? A Guide to Identifying Your Family's Strengths and Weaknesses.* New York: Brunner/Mazel, 1979.

Richardson, Ronald W. *Creating a Healthier Church: Family Systems Theory, Leadership, and Congregational Life.* Minneapolis: Augsburg Fortress, 1996.

Steinke, Peter L. *Healthy Congregations: A Systems Approach.* Bethesda: Alban Institute, 1996.

———. *How Your Church Family Works: Understanding Congregations as Emotional Systems.* Bethesda: Alban Institute, 1993.

TWO

I Press on toward the Goal

Competence as Self-Motivation

"Now what?"

Pastor Ellen Kramer sat down behind her desk and looked around her. It was 8:30 a.m. on the second Monday of her first pastorate. Her first week had been a whirlwind. Ellen loved doing details, and there had been a thousand to take care of. Now her books were in order, her favorite pictures were hung in her office, and she was duly installed and celebrated. Yesterday's marathon of service and reception had been one of the most affirming experiences of Ellen's life.

"We need you so much!" that silver-haired woman whose name Ellen couldn't yet remember had said. "No offense, but Pastor John just never did anything. We really did feel he worked just one day a week. I can tell you'll be a real self-starter. I just know you'll be the pastor we need!"

Unfortunately, she hadn't been the only one to say something along those lines. From the selection committee, the church elders, and a dozen get-acquainted conversations with members, Ellen got the same story. "Pastor John never worked. We felt cheated the whole time he was our pastor."

Ellen had met John Satterquist during the selection process. To her he'd seemed an intelligent, engaged, competent minister. He'd talked about the church with affection, except for "a few chronic complainers." When she asked for his advice, he had said, "Just be their pastor. Just love them and they'll love you."

Now she was really confused. She realized that nothing in her theological training had ever told her, beyond the obvious, precisely what a pastor does. "What makes a good pastor, anyway?" she wondered. "Is it what we are, or what we do? How aggressive should I be? What do I do today?"

21

Competence and Self-Motivation

The parish ministry is different from most jobs. Beyond preaching Sunday's sermon, celebrating communion, attending board meetings, and conducting baptisms, weddings, and funerals there is little consensus about precisely what a minister should do. Indeed, at least in American Protestant life, there is a perennial cultural joke that a minister "only works one day a week." That joke is based on the reality that ministerial work resists being quantified or measured. Many ministers do have a good bit of time many weeks which they must structure for themselves. When pastors spend all the unstructured office time in a given week reading, have they done their job? Maybe, maybe not.

I contend that a pastor needs both to be and to be seen to be self-motivated. By self-motivation I mean a competent pastor is energized from within on a daily basis to take the initiative in doing ministry. Self-motivation comes from your sense of God's call in your life. It comes both from who you are and from who you want to become.

How to achieve and cultivate self-motivation is a problem with at least four aspects: perception, personality, drive, and planning. It's a problem of perception because, in order to be thought of as competent by the congregation, a pastor must be perceived to be busy about the work of ministry. Americans are possessed of a profound and enduring allegiance to the Protestant work ethic. In the early years of the twenty-first century, studies show many of us actually work more hours a week than our parents did thirty years ago. We'll come back to this same issue several times in this book, especially in the chapters on time management and stress management. Achieving self-motivation is a problem of personality because many of the most visible aspects of a pastor's work, e.g. visitation and socializing, come easily to some of us and less easily to others. Drive, the will to succeed, is of course what most people think of when they think of self-motivation. Nobody wants to be a failure, but some seem more able to translate their wish for success into action.[1] Achieving self-motivation is a problem of planning, finally, because regardless of job description a minister must take personal responsibility for planning his or her own work.

When senior ministry students from my school's Readiness for Ministry colloquium talk about the importance of self-motivation, they naturally tend to talk in terms of what they have achieved thus far in their lives. Many of them have achieved a great deal. Their comments on the subject seem almost dismissive. "Look at what I've done so far. Of course I will be active and highly motivated as a minister." In assuming that they will be self-motivated in ministry, however, they overlook one essential dynamic. Unlike a course of study, for the most part the ordained ministry lacks a clear set of tasks, the accomplishment of which constitutes success.

I know, for example, of a minister who has just left a prosperous rural church for a new assignment after what he regarded as a successful multi-year ministry. What he does not know is that his parishioners were deeply dissatisfied with his work. "He spent too much time in the office, working on that computer!" they say. "We wanted him to visit more, to show an interest in our daily lives." It never seems to have occurred to him that what he viewed as necessary study and preparation, they viewed as neglect of the "real" work of the ministry. Clearly he was not self-motivated to discover and live out his congregation's expectations of a pastor.

[handwritten marginal note: what if their expectations are wrong ... aren't part of my responsibility?]

The question we need to address, then, has several parts. Where does our motivation for ministry originate? How is it expressed in the context of daily routine? What is the relationship between self-motivation and leadership for a minister? How do you know if what you want to do and what your congregation wants you to do are compatible? How do you gauge and cultivate your own motivation for your work?

Where Does Motivation for Ministry Originate?

Ministry is first of all a calling. It is a calling that has professional aspects and that requires professionalism, but at bottom the only sufficient reason to enter and to remain in the Christian ministry is the call of God. That has been true from the time Jesus told Peter to "Follow me!" The concept of calling means that ministerial self-motivation contains an irreducible rationale that is beyond the rational. When the apostle Paul says, "Woe to me if I do not preach the gospel!" (1 Cor. 9:16 RSV), he speaks for generations of his spiritual descendants who share a holy compulsion to serve.

Yet that fire has often burned low in the bones of those called. The *Didache,* the well known second-century manual for new Christians, contains a famous passage cautioning the church against itinerant prophets who stay too long, living off the church's hospitality. An early Lutheran document complained bitterly that many pastors drank too much. "It was frequently reported that preachers spent their time sitting around in taverns, and that many of them had the habit of staying at wedding parties until the last keg of beer was consumed."[2] Every seasoned church member has stories about pastors who spent more time on the golf course, albeit building relationships with members, or running their mail-order cleaning-supply business than they spent in visitation or sermon preparation.

George Herbert's *The Country Parson,* on the other hand, provides an idealized description of the English parish priest of the seventeenth century. Every day is to be spent in teaching, preaching, visiting, and doing good works. On Sunday, "having read divine Service twice fully, and preached in the morning and catechized in the afternoon . . . [t]he rest of the day he spends either reconciling neighbors that are at variance, or in visiting the sick, or in exhortations to some of his flock by themselves, whom his Sermons cannot or do not reach."[3] "A pastor," he declares, "is the Deputy of Christ for the reducing of Man to the Obedience of God."[4] That holy task requires nothing less than utter devotion.

The minister's character must be above reproach. "The Country Parson is exceeding exact in his Life, being holy, just, prudent, temperate, bold, grave in all his ways."[5] One might argue that few ministers in any era have attained such perfection! Too many pastors nearly kill themselves and neglect their families striving for an unrealistic ideal. Indeed, history shows that Herbert himself died early. For Herbert, though, whatever the details, it is the parson's status as deputy of Christ that pervades and motivates everything one does.

The theme of divine calling is perhaps the single constant that has unified American ministry across denominations and through the decades. As the ministry has declined in social status and intellectual respectability through the twentieth century and into the early twenty-first, once widely held cultural reasons for becoming a minister, such as security and prestige in the community, have largely evaporated. The ministry has come to be seen more as what it in fact is, a difficult and demanding occupation.

The Presbyterian writer Frederick Buechner famously tells of the response of a New York socialite to his confession that he had decided to become a minister: "Is this your own idea, or have you been poorly advised?"[6] The result of its decline in social status is that ministry is now in many ways what it was in the beginning, a task that one undertakes only when compelled to do so by the call of God. The specific content of that motivation may be self-described somewhat differently depending upon whether one's theological leanings are fundamentalist, evangelical, or mainline. Most serious ministers would though, I believe, affirm the senior student who wrote,

> I take my calling seriously and desire to be the best servant I can be. . . . Paul writes, "Whatever you do, work at it with all your heart, as working for the Lord, not for men." . . . My desire is to be always working for the Lord.[7]

If you're working for the Lord rather than for the church board, that constitutes self-motivation. If you're working for the board, it's time to search again for God's call in your life.

Self-Motivation and Daily Routine

Even when we're clear about our motivation for becoming a parish pastor, we still need to develop strategies for bridging the gap between the power of God's call and the practical challenges of the daily grind. Now we come to Pastor Ellen's issue. By and large, nobody structures our day for us. In his poetic little book *The Art of Pastoring*, Baptist pastor David Hansen describes his morning in a rural pastorate in Montana:

> My face sinks into my hands, but the desk is too cold for my elbows. The space heater with the cloth-covered cord has warmed the air: my breath doesn't show, but the steel desk warms excruciatingly slowly. It's freezing me. I'm too cold to read a book.

My office is a lean-to attachment to the fellowship hall of a community church in rural Montana. There's no wall heater, no thermostat, no insulation. The place warms from scratch every morning. It's six weeks into the new year, six weeks into my first pastoral charge, 33 degrees outside and sleeting.

It's sleeting in my soul. I don't know what I'm supposed to do. I've been called, educated, interned, and ordained. I have learned lists of tasks to do, but not what I am to *be*. I'm cold and afraid. There are a hundred things I could do if I could just stop shivering.[8]

Minus Hansen's office-insulation issues, it is precisely this point at which many of us fail to translate our training into action. The question, of course, is "Why?" Some might call this failure a lack of motivation or just plain laziness. Sloth, after all, does hold a place as one of the seven deadly sins.

I don't think so. My argument, based heavily on my own 20 years as a pastor, is that the primary culprit for this failure by otherwise hardworking ministers is personality type, our basic approaches to all of life's opportunities and challenges. How does our personality affect the way we manage our daily routine? Put yourself for a moment in Ellen's or David's place. You're just beginning your pastor-ate. It's not sermon-preparation day. You can do anything you like. The day stretches before you. If you had your preference of all the possible ministerial tasks you might undertake today, what would you most likely choose to do?

That lack of a prescribed routine, it seems to me, is precisely the challenge. Because nobody tells us most of the time what we have to do, most of us tend to do first the things we want to do. As an intense introvert, I never *wanted* to go visiting in the nursing homes. I would have much preferred to stay in my office and work on the week's sermon about compassion. If I waited to go visiting in the nursing homes until I felt like going visiting, it would never have happened. So I set one afternoon a week as my regular time to go. Over a period of weeks, I would see every long-term-care resident in the congregation. (It was a large congregation.) Then I'd start the rounds again. Because I went, a lot of ministry happened along the way, and much to my surprise I got the reputation of being a faithful pastoral visitor. But if I had not devised a routine for myself, I would never have made the visits.

My problem, of course, was exactly the opposite of that of many ministers. Some people are drawn to the ministry precisely because they love being with other people. They'll spend the whole week in one encounter after another, and come to Saturday evening with only the ghost of an idea about the next day's sermon. Whereas I had to discipline myself to get out of the office, many pastors need to discipline themselves to stay in. It's tough to get excited about filling out reports, working on plans for the new Sunday-school year, composing your column for the church newsletter, or checking three commentaries to be sure your have the right exegesis of a Greek word. But all those things are a necessary part of what we do.

In structuring a minister's day, then, a significant factor in self-motivation involves knowing yourself well enough to know which ministerial tasks you prefer, and which you are likely to put off. Knowing the specific tasks of ministry isn't the issue. Those don't really change radically from setting to setting, though they are obviously shaped to accommodate various congregational cultures. The issue, rather, is "How do you ensure that needful attention is paid, whether you particularly want to do the task or not?"

Temperament theory may apply to churches as well as to individuals. For example, one church I served was filled with strongly extroverted members. In addition, most of them assumed that the past determined the present and future, that feelings trumped thinking, and that decisions could be put off indefinitely. In short, I served an ESFP congregation. I am an ISTJ, at the opposite end of the temperament continuum. Once I recognized the distance between our temperaments, I altered my daily routine and behavior patterns to connect better with my church members. To love them well, I had to become more visible, emotionally transparent, and patient with the pace of decision-making. To borrow a concept from the world of Christian missions, think of this kind of process as "contextualizing" pastoral ministry. MAS

There's no substitute for the daily work of deciding what you will do. The best help, though, comes from fearless self-examination. We all have preferences, ways we prefer to work, strengths, and weaknesses. There's nothing wrong with that. But unless you know yourself well enough to be able to articulate which tasks come easily for you and which you'd prefer to avoid, it's difficult to make good decisions about your schedule. In the assessment section of the chapter, I suggest ways to develop the self-knowledge required to choose tasks wisely.

Self-Motivation and Vision

At first glance, the relationship between self-motivation and vision may seem obvious. "Self-motivation" is what we do for ourselves. "Vision" is what we convey to others. The reality, however, is more complex.

A competent minister is first of all a convinced and dedicated disciple of Jesus Christ. Any motivation or vision for ministry is rooted in the minister's relationship with Christ. In his letter to the church at Philippi, Paul talks about his own motivation for continuing his ministry specifically and for living the Christian life in general. "[B]ut this one thing I do: forgetting what lies behind and straining forward to what lies ahead, I press on toward the goal for the prize of the heavenly [upward] call of God in Christ Jesus" (Phil. 3:13-14). For Paul it is this passionate sense of his personal journey with Christ that keeps him going in the midst of difficulties. I believe this personal quest is true of any minister worthy of the name.

A significant part any minister's daily self-motivation simply must be the daily walk with Christ. Pentecostals talk about the leadership and empowering of the Holy Spirit when they describe this process. Pietists tend to speak of a daily devotional time. Martin Luther famously declared, "I have so much business I cannot get it done unless I pray three hours every day."

Centrality of prayer is the office of pastor

Quite prosaically then, the first answer to Ellen's "Now what?" should be "Pray. Seek God's guidance. Spend time daily seeking God's leadership for the day." Only ministry that flows out of an ongoing conversation between the believer and the Spirit of Christ will have the depth and durability to survive the rigors of pastoral life.

An excellent plan for Ellen, as she begins her work, would be to set up her calendar so that the first hour of the day is given to Scripture reading, prayer, and contemplation. It's important to keep this time separate from sermon preparation. Obviously there will be days when that is not possible. Demands seem always to hit as soon as the pastor walks in the door. But clear communication with the congregation (and your secretary) about your priority can help you stake out the time. Initially some might be irritated that you are not instantly available, but over time members and staff will come to appreciate and even depend on your faithfulness to this task.

A further aspect of our personal Christian walk deserves mention here. One of the greatest dangers ministers face is that of personal moral failure, straying across boundaries in their personal conduct or relationship with a parishioner. In addition to his or her personal relationship with Christ, every minister needs an accountability relationship with at least one other human being—a counselor, a colleague, or group of colleagues—someone with whom the minister can be both transparent and safe. Accountability, both spiritual and human, is essential to protect competent ministry. Early in your tenure, seek out a professional counselor whom you can consult as needed about personal matters. Look for a colleague in ministry with whom you can build a trust relationship. Seek to form a prayer and support group of pastors. In this way you create for yourself safe places to reveal your struggles and to be held accountable for your choices. Many pastors who cross boundaries do so in part because they have operated as "lone rangers." It's critical to connect yourself with others with whom you can be honest.

Second, though, a competent minister should seek and be able to articulate a vision of where God is leading the church he or she serves. Vision is unique to each congregation. It's derived from a combination of the church's circumstances and a sense of how God wants to work in and through those circumstances. A downtown church may develop a vision of ministry to the urban poor. A church near a college campus could find its vision in ministry to young adults. A minister seeks a vision by asking such questions as "What does God want to do in and through this church where and as we are?" You ask those questions of yourself, the congregation, the community, and God. Usually, out of those conversations, a vision will begin to emerge.

This vision, based in a faithful examination of reality, can then become a daily impetus for a minister's work. We'll talk more about leadership in a later chapter. Leadership is skill in the practical implementation of a vision. My point here is that the same sense of vision that makes for a good leader also makes for a self-motivated minister.

Vision will determine my taste ... getting the vision rolling

If I were Ellen, beginning that new pastorate, my answer to the "Now what?" question would be to <u>seek to identify a vision for the church</u>. In traditions in which a church chooses its own pastor, discussion of a church's vision is often part of the candidacy process. Even in appointive systems, though, the bishop or district superintendent will seek to discover the right person for a church's needs and direction at a given point in time. <u>Where vision is unclear, leading the church to discover and articulate its vision can be the most fruitful possible work of the first couple of years of a pastorate</u>. Going through the process of vision casting provides an opportunity for a pastor and congregation to get to know one another, to develop trust, and to affirm shared goals.

Very often the best way to help a church develop its vision is to enter into a strategic planning process. A committee is chosen rep-resenting the various significant constituencies in the church—age groups, ministry areas, elders and deacons, and so forth. This committee then seeks input from all branches of the church family. From that input the committee distills a set of priorities for the next three to five years of the church's life. This set of priorities is then discussed, adjusted, and adopted by the church as a whole. These priorities, often concentrated into a single sentence, become the church's vision for its corporate life. Without dictating the process or its outcome, the pastor is

---

When I came to Trinity, it was clear that the congregation needed a vision. But it was, at first, difficult to discern where to begin. Even before holding small-group meetings to talk about the congregation—meetings that were not always well attended—I had many people dropping ideas and comments about the congregation, their hopes, their ideas, the current program. For some months, as each idea came forward, I wrote each on a small blue slip of paper. I pinned each two-by-two-inch paper (with such words as "St. Joan of Arc," "youth group," "basketball hoop," "hunger outreach," "women's retreat," and so forth, written on them) on a bulletin board. This action did two things for me: It gave me a sense of control over all the ideas and suggestions that were being virtually thrown at me. I had them all in one place where I could see them. It also allowed me to begin to see patterns of interest, need, and categories. I was less overwhelmed than I might otherwise have been. It helped me to know where to begin as I included the ideas with all the comments from small-group meetings. JM

involved at every stage of the planning process. He or she then becomes the chief articulator of the vision. The vision is referred to regularly in sermons, in committee work, and as the governing board meets and makes decisions. The pastor keeps the vision constantly before the church.

When I went to my fourth pastorate, in an older church in a stable urban neighborhood, the church desperately needed to refocus its vision. I led the church into a strategic planning process that identified a set of priorities for the next three to five years of its ministry. That strategic plan then became one motivating structure for my daily work. It was always possible to go to the office in the morning and ask myself, "What should I do today to help us toward where we want to go?"

[handwritten margin note: STRATEGIC PLANNING help determine task]

There is of course a third aspect of the connection between self-motivation and vision: the natural reinforcement that develops when church members see us living out our vision for the church *and begin to live out that vision in their lives as well.* Nothing else in my pastorates was as motivating to me as realizing that someone else had "caught on" to where the Lord was leading the church and was beginning to act on that vision. In a church with a vision of reaching out to its community, members began to come to me with ideas for new initiatives. Often they simply took action on their own. This kind of reaction isn't likely to happen in the first few years in a pastorate. It may not happen at all. But when it does come, it strengthens our own motivation for our work as perhaps nothing else can do.

Self-Motivation Strategies

If you want to develop a better understanding of, and to improve, your self-motivation for ministry, how do you go about it? The rest of the chapter offers a few personal strategies.

Know Your Type

Obviously there is a difference between wanting to succeed in the ministry and doing the things one must do to become a competent minister. A key component is self-knowledge. Most seminaries require students to take a battery of tests to help them understand their personality, personal maturity, and potential for ministry. Schools vary a good deal in the use they make of this information.

I contend that all ministerial candidates should take some version of the Myers-Briggs Type Indicator, and take the time to learn enough about their own type to begin to see how their personality type influences their actions. Most ministerial professionals these days are familiar with the Myers-Briggs Type Indicator inventories.

In effect, the Myers-Briggs Type Indicator teaches that our personalities lie along four continua. These are: (1) Introversion to Extraversion, (2) Intuitive to Sensing, (3) Thinking to Feeling, and (4) Perceiving to Judging.

A person who takes the test receives a four-letter profile indicating where he or she falls among the 16 possible types. Your profile suggests how you process information and make decisions. The Myers-Briggs test has several advantages. It is easy to use. It translates complicated concepts into relatively simple terms. It emphasizes the fluidity of personality, and it is an excellent tool for helping people understand themselves as "hardwired" for a certain set of preferences. In this way, for many people, it becomes a vehicle of grace. JAH

These simple preference tests help people discover how they make their decisions and where they get and spend energy. Some of us are extroverts. Some of us are introverts. Some of us like tasks. Some of us like experiences. Some of us like to get things done. Some of us like to gather input. By discovering your Myers-Briggs type, you gain a useful tool in understanding your own actions and preferences.

The MBTI is best administered and interpreted by those who are trained for the purpose. In their book *Please Understand Me*, however, Keirsey and Bates provide an abbreviated version of the MBTI that can be self-scored and that includes sufficient interpretive information to help you discover your Myers-Briggs type.[9]

If you do know your type, think about the aspects of your personality that may influence your daily choices as you structure your time as a minister. Many youth ministers, for example, identify their type as ENFP. (If you're unfamiliar with Myers-Briggs, feel free to take a trip to the bookstore or library now.) ENFPs enjoy spending time with people. They love new experiences. They respond to emotion. They're much more interested in experiencing life and enjoying people than in getting things done. I know people whose type is ENFP and who function brilliantly in administrative ministries. But they will tell you that it doesn't come without struggle. They have had to learn to pay attention to the myriad organizational details that would come easily to a person of a different type.

I, on the other hand, as an ISTJ (the opposite personality type), tend to think that the task comes before the relationship. I'd rather go home early and get to bed so that I can be on time for work in the morning. As a pastor, I had to learn to pay attention to people, experiences, and feelings.

Similarly, a pastor who is a J, the kind of person who likes to get things done, may get frustrated working with a committee dominated by Ps, the kind of folk who always want to gather more information. A pastor who is a J may contemplate homicide when working with a youth minister who is a P. Congregations generally expect their pastors to be NFs, intuitive feelers, the kind of people who see the big picture and are extraordinarily sensitive to others' feelings. Pastors of other types may be perceived as aloof, uncaring, or rigid. The point here is not that we must change our type to suit the ministerial ideal. The point is that by being aware of our type, we can adjust our behavior to compensate for our natural preferences. Being an ISTJ is not an excuse for staying in your office and avoiding people. Being an ENFP is not an excuse for never getting your sermon done. The sooner you know your own type and how people of your type tend to respond, the better job you can do of shaping your day to provide a well-rounded ministry.

How precisely does knowing your type relate to self-motivation? The Christian psychologist Scott Peck defined original sin as laziness, the unwillingness to exert ourselves to grow or change.[10] When you know and understand your personality type, you have the opportunity to shape your daily activities in the direction of balanced, effective ministry. A minister who is seeking to follow Christ will want to work effectively.

Cultivate Your Christian Walk

The single most important element in protecting your motivation for ministry is pursuing your own day-to-day relationship with Christ. Far too many ministers become mere functionaries, doing the tasks of the church without practicing the substance of the faith, which is that personal relationship. Assessing where you are in practicing the faith isn't really difficult. Chances are, you learned most of the basic Christian disciplines in confirmation class or Sunday school. Here's a refresher though, with a focus on the ministry. Answer yes or no to the following questions:

- Do you have a daily time for Bible reading and prayer apart from your sermon preparation?   Y N
- Are you currently reading some work of Christian literature?   Y N
- Do you subscribe to a professional journal for ministers?   Y N
- Are you part of an accountability/peer group you trust?   Y N
- Do you have an ongoing relationship with a mentor/spiritual director?   Y N
- Do you seek the Holy Spirit's companionship in your daily walk?   Y N
- Do you have a place to go if you need personal/spiritual counsel?   Y N
- Do you worship regularly outside your place of responsibility?   Y N
- Is Christ teaching you something new?   Y N
- Is God still calling you to serve in this place?   Y N

The more "yes" answers you give, the better your daily walk with Christ, and the better your motivation for ministry should be. You should feel a sense of energy and purpose as your walk with Christ lends meaning to each day. In effect, you're living out your ministry in partnership with Christ rather than on your own.

Many of us have a particularly difficult time choosing meaningful devotional reading. It's quite easy to get through most M.Div. curricula without ever treating the subject seriously. Accordingly, I've provided below a personal list of some of the best and most interesting Christian devotional literature from throughout the history of the church. The list, arranged in roughly chronological order, is not intended to be exhaustive. It does intentionally neglect popular devotional material of the late twentieth and early twenty-first centuries. The publishers of those volumes will work quite hard enough to persuade you that their products are classics without any assistance from me!

Saint Augustine, *Confessions*
————, *City of God*
Saint Francis of Assisi, *The Little Flowers of Saint Francis*
Juliana of Norwich, *Revelations of Divine Love*
Saint Teresa of Avila, *The Life of Teresa of Jesus*
Saint John of the Cross, *Dark Night of the Soul*
George Herbert, *The Country Parson*
John Bunyan, *The Pilgrim's Progress*
Philip Jacob Spener, *Pia Desideria*
William Law, *A Serious Call to a Devout and Holy Life*
C. S. Lewis, *Mere Christianity*
————, *Surprised by Joy*
————, *The Problem of Pain*
————, *The Great Divorce*
————, *The Screwtape Letters*
————, The Chronicles of Narnia
————, The Space Trilogy *(Perelandra, That Hideous Strength, Out of the Silent Planet)*
Dietrich Bonhoeffer, *The Cost of Discipleship*
————, *Life Together*
————, *Letters and Papers from Prison*
Thomas Merton, *The Seven-Story Mountain*
————, *Thoughts in Solitude*
Elton Trueblood, *A Place to Stand*
Henri Nouwen, *The Wounded Healer*
Richard Foster, *A Celebration of Discipline*
————, *Prayer*
Frederick Buechner, *The Sacred Journey*
————, *Wishful Thinking*
————, *Listening to Your Life*

I've left out any number of classics. The Scriptures, first and foremost, come to mind. Surprisingly few pastors read the Bible at all except to prepare sermons. Still, with the list above, I'm confident that you can find help that stretches your world and points you toward deeper devotion.

Another difficult problem for many of us is finding an accountability or peer group with which we can be comfortable. Some denominations create such groups geographically. At other times they
develop from lectionary study groups or prayer groups that ministers establish on their own. I believe the best strategy is to select a
group of three or four colleagues who covenant together to be a
support for one another. Such a group should operate under a pledge
of confidentiality, with a proviso that the group has the right to suggest
that any member get professional counseling when necessary.

Seeking a mentor or spiritual director, from my perspective, is a
more difficult issue. I want my mentor to be someone further along
the spiritual journey than I. I want this person to be trained in some form of counseling as well as in spiritual direction. I want to feel confident that, when the mentor speaks to me, he or she speaks for Christ, with my well-being in mind. Ask yourself, "Of all the people I know, whose counsel would I most like to seek on a regular basis?" Then ask that person to consider becoming your spiritual mentor.

While I was in seminary, I also served as a lay professional at a congregation. I was a single parent with two teenage sons. I went to school full time, worked a 30-hour week, and maintained home and family. I was so tired! I wished so much just to stay home from our church council retreat so I'd get a good night's sleep. But I had responsibilities for the program and went to the camp. The weekend was full of laughter and good fun. I stayed up much later than I might have at home but discovered that being relaxed and laughing was a tonic as valuable as sleep itself. I returned refreshed and renewed with energy for work and school and family. JM

As for worshiping regularly outside your own context of service, I appreciate how difficult that can be. I have one colleague who slips over regularly to the Saturday evening service in a large congregation of another denomination. The anonymity and the different liturgy provide him with the safety and stimulation he needs to worship. Some ministers write into their contracts periodic Sundays off for worship. Others watch one of the TV preachers, go on monthly one-day retreats, or arrange to alternate worship leadership responsibilities with a neighboring pastor. The key is that you find a regular way to be a member of the congregation rather than the leader.

Ideally, the checklist above should be seen not as a way to grade your spirituality but as a stimulus to growth. If you answered no to one or more of the questions, why not devise a plan to move your no to yes?

Know When to Get Help

Perhaps your particular lack of self-motivation is more complex than anything we've yet mentioned. More than any other issue in this book, loss of motivation can slip upon us unaware and can come from a multitude of directions—health, overwork, family issues, the working of the Spirit, or grief, to name a few. The real trouble with self-motivation, ultimately, is that you are responsible for your own. Most often, we don't find ourselves thinking about the concept of self-motivation until we've lost it—and that tendency, in turn, makes it difficult to muster the energy to change!

Many times the answer to loss of motivation is quite simple. We need rest, retreat, or vacation, a short-term recharging of the batteries. In that sense ministers are no different from bank tellers or physicians. Everybody needs to get away now and then. The question here is "How do I know when my loss of motivation is more serious?"

Below you'll find a simple set of questions designed to help you think about whether it's time you talked with someone about your motivation. Answer yes or no to the following. The more yes answers you give, the more likely you need to consult a mentor or a counselor about your motivation for ministry.

- I have trouble sleeping these days.   Y N
- I feel tired all the time.   Y N
- Often I sit in my office and do nothing for long periods. Y N
- My prayer life seems to be deteriorating.   Y N
- I've been losing (or gaining) a lot of weight lately.   Y N
- I don't know what direction to lead our church next.   Y N
- I wish people would just leave me alone.   Y N
- I'm really angry with the church or its leaders.   Y N
- I'm not taking good care of myself, and I know it.   Y N

- There are huge parts of my job I don't enjoy.   Y N
- I always look for ways to spend time outside the church.   Y N

Any of us may have days when more than one of these statements is true. But if a significant portion of the list is consistently true for you, if you're not getting up and going to work most mornings glad and grateful for the ministry God has given you, it's time to talk with someone you trust. Put down the book and make an appointment now! You *can* feel better!

The most basic truth of ministry is that we are not alone. The Christ who sends us wants not only to walk beside us but also to provide us with the companionship and support of others that we need to maintain our enthusiasm. By making use of the right resources we can keep ourselves healthy and growing both personally and in our work.

In the end, self-motivation for ministry is defined as taking personal responsibility for who we are becoming and what we are doing as servants of Christ. It involves our commitment to Christ, our understanding of ourselves and of our calling, and our determination to live out that calling with integrity and purpose.

Further Reading

In addition to those works already cited, you might find considerable help thinking through issues of motivation in the following works:

Belasic, David S., and Paul M. Schmidt. *The Penguin Principles: A Survival Guide for Clergy Seeking Maturity in Ministry.* Lima, Ohio: CSS Publishing Co., 1986.

Galloway, John Jr. *Ministry Loves Company: A Survival Guide for Pastors.* Louisville: Westminster John Knox, 2003.

Johnson, Spencer. *Who Moved My Cheese?* New York: G. P. Putnam's Sons, 1998.

THREE

If the Trumpet Gives an Uncertain Sound

Competent Communication Skills

"Eleanor, of course I didn't mean that. . . . I do know how painful this is for you, and I'm truly sorry you didn't feel my concern. . . . OK, let's talk again in a couple of days. . . . God bless you. Goodbye!"

Mark hung up the phone in a cold sweat. That was his third irate call of the morning. For the hundredth time, he wished for a videotape ministry. At least then he could find out what he'd said. Today, though, if he had a videotape, he might want to erase it.

As one who preached without notes, Mark made it a practice to avoid writing any kind of manuscript for his sermons. Each week he gathered his notes, put them in order, spoke through the sermon aloud several times to fix his ideas and the flow of logic in his mind, and then took nothing but the Bible into the pulpit with him.

Apparently, though, he'd made a real mistake. In yesterday's sermon about truth-telling, he'd used an illustration describing how a woman had falsely accused a man of rape; then, after becoming a Christian years later, changed her testimony and saw to it that the man was set free. A few people had somehow gotten the idea that he was discouraging abuse victims from reporting the abuse! He knew he hadn't intended to say any such thing, but he also knew the power of impressions. Giving comfort to abusers was the last thing he wanted to do. What a mess! More important, what should he do now?

Issue: Competence in Communication

Anyone who's ever played the children's game called "Gossip" knows how difficult it is to communicate clearly. The first person speaks a simple sentence into the second person's ear. The second person repeats what she heard to the third. By the time the sentence travels around the room, it's altered beyond all recognition. Mark, in the vignette above, is by no means alone. Many a hopeful ship of ministry sets sail only to founder on the rock of poor communication.

Part of the problem here is that we ministers tend to think we do a better job of communicating than we do. We're continually surprised when church folk aren't aware of the new program we've been talking about for weeks, or don't know about the issue we discussed so carefully in the newsletter. Especially we seem to think we're better preachers than we are. Senior students at the seminary where I serve consistently rate the ability to preach well as one of their strongest assets as they leave seminary. As their professor of homiletics, my observation is that some of them can and some of them can't. This tendency to think better of our abilities than others do is apparently nothing new. A quarter-century ago Methodist researcher Steve Clapp conducted an extensive survey of clergy and laity from a cross-section of American denominations. He discovered that "Ministers and active church members evaluate pastoral skill in the pulpit in a different way. Most ministers covered by our surveys and interviews felt that clergy do a good or excellent job conducting worship and preaching. Their active church members were considerably less enthusiastic."[1] Congregations want sermons that are faithful to the Scriptures and that speak directly to their lives. This kind of relevance, Clapp observes, is considered important by worshipers whether we are talking about liberal or conservative congregations.[2]

While good communication from the pulpit is clearly important, Clapp makes one other observation that points us in our next direction. In talking with nonmembers of the congregations he surveyed, Clapp found that few of them were drawn to the church because of the quality of the preaching. Instead it was the quality of personal relationships offered by the clergy and the laity.[3] To put it bluntly, people don't join because we preach well. They join because we care about them and because we communicate our caring in ways they can appreciate. And again, we often think we communicate our caring better than we actually do. Churches in my tradition, for example, frequently greet visitors on Sunday morning by having the members stand in their honor, while the visitors remain seated. This practice allows the ushers to identify visitors quickly and to give them a packet of information about the church. Unfortunately this kind of greeting fails to recognize that many visitors are acutely uncomfortable with being singled out in any way. We don't communicate the caring we intend.

This need to express ourselves in caring ways means, in part, that we ministers must cultivate competence in personal communication. I come from a rather blunt family. One consequence is that I'm not always aware of the tone of voice I use, or of the way that tone is perceived by others. In one church, an older woman was in the habit of helping in the church office on Sunday mornings. One Sunday, under the pressures of the morning, I apparently spoke curtly to her. For me it was a passing moment. I still don't remember doing so. But for her it became evidence of my lack of respect toward her. She resented me for years before I ever heard the story. Clearly both what we say and how we say it can and do affect our relationships with our people.

Personal communication, of course, is also reflected in the way we teach. A pastor who is a good teacher can communicate respect and gentleness, can give her people permission to grow as Christians and to think for themselves. A teaching pastor who is nervous about his own abilities, who is more concerned with delivering the "right" answer than with encouraging his people to think, can effectively shut down a group's potential for growth. Not long a go I watched a young pastor teach the adult Sunday school class in his church. Several times during the lesson, he asked a question and immediately answered it himself. What was communicated? "I don't trust you folks to come up with an appropriate answer!"

Another significant aspect of communication takes place in the pastor's writing. Most ministers, I'd guess, don't think of their written communication with the congregation as particularly important. The truth is that a ministry isn't likely to stand or fall on the basis of your column in the church newsletter. Still, it's a mistake to underestimate the potential for good or ill in what you write. The director of our summer day-care program once sent a letter to parents explaining that the kids' swimming pool trip had been cut short because of a problem of "deification" in the pool. Aside from being exceedingly dubious theologically, and silly enough to make a national pundit's "church bloopers" column, the mistake helped undermine folks' already shaky confidence in her competence. In fact, how you say what you say matters. It matters every time. It matters in every setting. In many ways communication is a minister's most essential tool.

Competent Ministerial Communication

Factors in competent communication include the character of the minister, the quality of caring that is communicated, and the skill with which a presentation is made. These factors come into play regardless of the arena in which communication is attempted. Typical arenas for communication include pastoral care, teaching, administration, and preaching.

The first factor in competent ministerial communication doesn't necessarily involve words at all. It is the element of the pastor's character as that character is experienced by the congregation. By character I mean a person's habits of behavior and approach toward life.

In Paul's first letter to the Thessalonians, he reminds them of the posture of his ministry:

> But we were gentle among you, like a nurse tenderly caring for her own children. So deeply do we care for you that we are determined to share with you not only the gospel of God but also our own selves, because you have become very dear to us. You remember our labor and toil, brothers and sisters; we worked night and day, so that we might not burden any of you while we proclaimed to you the gospel of God. You are witnesses, and God also, how pure, upright, and blameless our conduct was toward you believers.
>
> 1 Thessalonians 2:7b-10

Part of what Paul is saying here is that his manner of life was designed to communicate to the Thessalonians the sincerity of his faith. You and I also find this true in our ministries whether or not we want it to be so.

Our lives as demonstrated in our attitudes and behaviors either validate or invalidate our professions. George Herbert writes of the country parson:

> The Country Parson is exceeding exact in his Life, being holy, just, prudent, temperate, bold, grave in all his ways. And because the two highest points of Life, wherein a Christian is most seen, are Patience, and Mortification; Patience in regard of afflictions, Mortification in regard of lusts and affections, and the stupifying and deading of all the clamorous powers of the soul, therefore he hath thoroughly studied these, that he may be an absolute Master and commander of himself, for all the purposes which God hath ordained him. Yet in these points he labors most in those things which are most apt to scandalize his Parish. And first, because Country people live hardly . . . the Country Parson is very circumspect in avoiding all covetousness, neither being greedy to get, nor niggardly to keep. . . . but in all his words and actions slighting and disesteeming it. . . . Secondly, because Luxury is a very visible sin, the Parson is very careful to avoid all the kinds thereof, but especially drinking because it is the most popular vice. . . . Thirdly, because Country people . . . do much esteem their word. . . . therefore the parson is very strict in keeping his word, though it be to his own hindrance, as knowing, that if he be not so, he will quickly be discovered, and disregarded; neither will they believe him in the pulpit, whom they cannot trust in his Conversation.[4]

That worthy English divine writing more than 350 years ago has it exactly right for the 21st century as well. We ministers communicate with our lives long before we climb into our pulpits. What we say with our lives speaks louder than anything we're likely to express in speech.

The fact that Herbert nailed the point so well so long ago hasn't, of course, kept practical theologians since then from trying to say it better. A similar point is made in different ways from the perspective of various disciplines within theological circles. United Methodist bishop, preacher, and theologian William Willimon argues for the continuing validity of the call to servanthood that Jesus gives in

Luke 22.[5] Catholic spiritual leader Henri Nouwen talks in terms of spirituality: "So ministry and spirituality never can be separated. Ministry is not an eight to five job but primarily a way of life which is for others to see and understand so that liberation can become a possibility."[6]

From a congregation's point of view, perhaps the most important factor about himself or herself that a minister must communicate is caring. Yale professor Gaylord Noyce, in his book *Pastoral Ethics,* quotes Nouwen extensively and summarizes by expanding on the idea that the minister is a "caring self" who demonstrates the twin characteristics of commitment and competence.[7] The classic pastoral care authority Wayne Oates talks in terms of the symbolic role of the pastor: "The sovereignty of God, the principle of incarnation whereby the word was made flesh, the activity of the Holy Spirit in contemporary living, and the function of the church as the body of Christ— these are the realities that the pastor symbolizes and represents."[8] I would argue that in their different ways each is saying something very similar to what Herbert said so long ago. Ministers communicate the gospel to the people first and foremost through their own lives. Along with their personal character, the caring way they walk among their people embodies for the people what their minister believes that following Christ means.

A competent pastor communicates caring. The real problem with Mark's sermon was that some in his congregation didn't hear the illustration he used as caring for the victims of abuse. Fair or not, that's what they heard. Whether we as pastors are preaching, teaching, writing, counseling, or simply involved in conver-

Try walking among the people before the start of the worship or Bible study hour. Take your time. Remember, you want people to intercept and talk with you. When someone does so, be sure to make eye contact and to listen intently. Many times, the conversation will be about the common stuff of life: weather, sports, work, the latest story about a grandchild and the like. On occasion, though, a person will take the opportunity to share some personal concern or need. Either kind of conversation is important. Many of those who talk with you would never have called the church office to make an appointment. Over time, you come to know church members far better than would have been the case had you never "walked the halls," and church members will believe you care for them. MAS

sation, we will be evaluated on the basis of how well we communicate caring. From this point of view, when we are with the congregation in any context, we are never "off duty." Everything we say or write will be evaluated with the question, "Does she really care about us?" The answer people give to that question will determine whether they believe you are a good pastor. Living out your own faith in your personal character and in the quality of your caring for your congregation are the first two factors in competent communication.

Readers should note that we're not without contemporary help in defining what pastoral character encompasses. Many denominations spell out their behavioral expectations for ordained ministers either in an official document such as the *United Methodist Book of Discipline* or in a code of ethics. Your denomination's expectations for your behavior can serve as a good starting point for personal evaluation.[9]

Preaching

The third major factor in any kind of communicating you do in the church is the skill with which you do it. Perhaps the most significant arena in which most pastors communicate with their congregation on a regular basis comprises the preaching task. It's impossible for a homiletics professor and former pastor to say all I'd like to say on this subject in the space allotted to this chapter. But I'll try!

The theologian Karl Barth places the proclamation of the gospel at the very center of the church's life and worship. He's famously quoted as saying that the preacher stands before the congregation with the Bible in one hand and the newspaper in the other. He's also quoted as saying, when asked the most important thing he'd learned as a theologian, the line from the old children's hymn, "Jesus loves me, this I know, for the Bible tells me so!" These three images from Barth seem to me to say something vital about competent communication through preaching.

First, preaching is at the center of the church's life. It is both bigger than we are as individuals and a vital part of what we do as pastors. Many people speak well who know nothing of Christ. But no one can consistently preach the gospel who has not been somehow transformed by that gospel. Preaching is therefore a participation in the work of the Spirit in shaping and forming Christ's church.

Second, preaching is necessarily contextual and ethical.[10] Preaching is meant to challenge and call to change a particular congregation in a particular place at a particular time. It holds our daily lives up to the light of Christ as revealed in Scripture and points us toward Christ's way. A preacher who tells only the scriptural story without using that Scripture to enlighten our stories is failing in the preaching task.

NEED for TRUE Delving into the WORD

Third, preaching is necessarily personal. Barth's reference to "Jesus Loves Me" is startling to many because of the voluminous extent of his written works and his exalted status as a theologian. What he's saying, though, is nothing less than the essence of the Christian story. When Tom Long, in his homiletics text, talks about the essential character of the preacher as witness, he hits upon this very point.[11] We who preach are talking about what has happened to us. If you don't know in the center of your being that Jesus loves you, then you as a preacher have nothing to say. If you do, then you have everything to say.

None of this essential authenticity, of course, means that you will be any good at all at saying what being a Christian is all about. Some of the most wonderful Christians I know can't string two words together competently. Clearly, in addition to our personal experience, several other elements need to be present for competent preaching communication. I'll confine myself to 10.

Competent preaching

1. *Sound biblical exegesis.* Christian faith and Christian preaching remain rooted in the Bible. Whatever one's theology of biblical authority may be, it's essential that the way we use Scripture in our preaching reflect an accurate understanding of the meaning of the text. That means a preacher must do the work of discovery.

Some seminaries no longer require study of biblical languages for the master of divinity degree. The ability to use commentaries and other secondary sources may be sufficient. The point, however, is that no preacher should ever assume to know what a text means without scholarly study—which leads us to our second point.

2. *Adequate weekly preparation time.* Competent preaching simply can't be done consistently without adequate preparation time:

time to think, read, pray, reflect, and plan what one intends to say. In my view you cannot possibly do this on Saturday night. The best preaching comes, I believe, when texts and themes are selected well in advance, study is done early in the week, and time for composition is built into a preacher's weekly schedule and protected. As a pastor, I told my people, "I write my sermons on Thursday. Please don't call or come by unless you genuinely need me." They learned to respect and value that preparation time.

Two additional expectations are implicit in this need for adequate preparation. The first is that a competent pastor does his or her own work. Plagiarism is inexcusable. The second is that a preacher takes the time to check sources and to be as certain as possible that what is said from the pulpit is accurate and true.

What is it though... Nothing new under the sun? —How?

3. *Variety in presentation*. One old joke about preaching is the tiresome quality of the "three points and a poem" form when repeated every Sunday. One cartoon shows a preacher saying, "As a corrective to last week's 26-point sermon, today's sermon will be pointless." I would argue that clarity and variety are twin poles of one axis of sermon preparation.

Competent preaching never confuses people. It may intrigue or puzzle in the beginning as a way to encourage listening. Creating a tension that is ultimately resolved is a time-tested technique. But the preacher must always provide sufficient structure to bring the congregation along with her. Saying "first, second, third" is sometimes considered out of fashion, but that is far better than leaving a congregation confused about the structure of what you're saying.

Narrative preaching, particularly, can be useful as a vehicle of pastoral care. In narrative preaching the preacher identifies the dominant myth in the biblical story to help us interpret our own story. Martin Luther King, Jr., for example, used the Hebrew exodus story as dominant myth—"Freedom Road"—as an interpretive vehicle for the civil rights struggle in America. In effect, the preacher retells the biblical story and then lays our own story beside it. The story becomes its own interpretation. The story itself may validate or confront our own experience. Narrative preaching emphasizes the importance of *kairos* moments in an individual's life or a people's history. These are times when converging streams merge or clash and out of the turmoil a new perspective, adjustment, or resolution is born. JAH

At the same time the preacher who wants people to listen will take care not to bore them by structuring the sermon in the same way every Sunday. Sermons can be inductive, deductive, narrative, dialogical, and so forth in virtually endless variety.

4. *Life application.* Competent preaching applies the truths of Scripture to the daily lives of the congregation. People want to know how to cope with their difficulties and to live successfully as Christians in the everyday world. They don't care, by and large, about biblical minutiae. As Harry Emerson Fosdick once observed, "Only the preacher proceeds still upon the idea that folk come to church desperate to discover what happened to the Jebusites."[12]

5. *Speech Skills.* Many seminaries offer an entire course in the specifics of sermon delivery. These courses address a wide variety of subjects, including proper breath control, the materials one takes into the pulpit, the importance of eye contact, enunciation, and projection. Put simply, how you speak your sermon should never be allowed to hamper the congregation's ability to hear what you are saying. Delivery should be designed and executed so as to enhance the opportunity for hearing.

The crucial point here is that no preacher ever finishes learning these skills. Mannerisms have a way of becoming habits. In almost every congregation, worshipers say things like, "Have you noticed that the preacher always looks to the left? What's wrong with those of us who sit on the right?" It's essential to submit ourselves to some kind of regular feedback on how we are doing what we do.

6. *Awareness of what needs to be said and the congregation's ability to hear it.* The need to be contextually appropriate goes back to Barth's "the Bible and the newspaper." A competent preacher keeps a finger on the pulse of popular culture. People bring with them to church whatever is going on in their day-to-day lives. If the Congress or the courts are struggling with a controversial issue, or if there has been some major national or local disaster, it is part of the preacher's responsibility to speak a gospel word to the situation. In addition, the very nature of the pastorate is such that the preacher will become aware over time of the major areas in which the congregation members need to grow in their faith. Failure to address those needs from the pulpit represents a failure of pastoral responsibility.

The only caveat here is a call for discernment. Some things people are ready to hear. Some things they're not ready to hear, even if those statements happen to be gospel truth. This is the point at which the preacher Mark in our opening vignette could have been more sensitive. His illustration was theologically and ethically correct. Yet it failed to take into account the struggle of many church folk to name and confront abuse. Mark underestimated the difficulty and the emotion connected with that struggle. He'd have been heard more clearly if he had used a different illustration.

A wise preacher challenges people to grow without turning them off completely. But aren't there times when we must speak the truth regardless of the consequences? Yes. I'm simply saying that we must choose those times carefully. My home pastor, who had been through the civil rights struggles in the South, put it this way: "Before you crawl up on a cross, make sure it's for the salvation of the world."

7. *Awareness of the worship culture.* These days preachers are presented with an ever-increasing array of tools to use in their delivery. These tools range from the recovery of ancient liturgies to the widespread use of video clips and PowerPoint computerized displays. Some congregations have considerable enthusiasm for the use of electronic media in worship, for example. Others have never experienced such a thing or want no part of it. The preacher's first strategy should be to mold his or her initial presentation style to the congregation's custom. Innovation can happen, but it should happen at a pace that allows the congregation to adjust to the change. The message itself is always primary. The rest is just packaging, and should never be allowed to detract from people's ability to receive the message.

8. *Passion.* By passion I don't mean shouting at people or getting angry or, worst of all, crying in the pulpit. I do mean caring obviously and deeply about what we are saying. Nobody else will take seriously what we don't take seriously ourselves. Tom Long observes, "If we are faithfully exercising our ministry of preaching, bearing witness to the gospel, for and with people whom we love, over time it will show. If we are fundamentally bored by what we are doing, feel contempt for or superior to the hearers, are cynical toward what we are preaching, try to be impressive or charming, or wish we were in some other vocation, that will also show."[13] I have heard technically correct, beautifully structured, immaculately presented sermons which left everyone concerned cold with indifference. I have heard technically lousy, badly presented sermons which touched

me and the rest of the congregation because the preacher obviously cared deeply about what was being said.

9. *Humor.* Humor provides the necessary balance to the preacher's passion. Humor disarms resistance, affirms that we are all in the same boat, and keeps us from taking ourselves more seriously than is healthy for us or the congregation. Only rarely does our humor involve telling a joke. Preachers are not to be stand-up comics. What we can do is point out the inherent humor in the human condition. Because laughter is emotional, it gives people permission to tap into their feelings in a way that a structured argument never can. Sermons without humor ignore one of the most powerful tools at the preacher's disposal.

10. *Prayer.* In preaching we cooperate with the Spirit in bringing God's word to the church. Stating the need to pray about our preaching might seem unnecessary. On the contrary, I think it is absolutely essential. To attempt to grow a sermon without prayer is like attempting to grow a tree without watering the seed. In prayer we submit our creative process to God's Spirit and ask for help both in hearing ourselves what needs to be said and in shaping that sermon for the congregation that will hear it. A good writer can craft a speech about biblical truth without submitting to the discipline of prayer. But it isn't a sermon until God is at work in the process.

Others would offer a different list of the elements in competent preaching. I have not mentioned doctrinal content, for example, or the importance of balancing evangelism, teaching, pastoral care, and congregational formation in one's preaching. I take the liberty of assuming that you know what you believe and that you're attempting to balance the overall diet offered in sermon fare. The list above is specific to the sermon itself and focused on the elements which I believe will make a specific sermon worth hearing.

Additional Arenas of Communication

Beyond the skill of the pastor's preaching lies the remainder of the pastor's interactions with parishioners, verbal and written, in committees, classes, and social situations. Every minister is different, of course. Some are wonderfully adept in working with committees but awkward in out-of-church social situations. Others work beautifully with small groups but freeze in front of large classes. Some, like Barbara Walters, can talk with practically anybody about practically anything. The technical components of competence in writing are very different from those in teaching. Again, whole courses are devoted to these subjects. I want simply to mention a few characteristics which all pastoral interactions with parishioners outside the pulpit should ideally share.

Competent communication requires adequate preparation. A great deal of pastoral work happens on the spur of the moment. We're called to a hospital bed, or the phone rings with a parishioner's question. Perhaps as a result of this reality, many pastors tend to develop a kind of "shoot from the hip" mentality about their interactions with the congregation.

It's important to recognize, though, that much of what we do can benefit from advance preparation. If you're teaching a class, that class deserves thoughtful consideration of how to achieve your learning goal. Your regular column in the newsletter is your chance to touch the minds of many church members with carefully considered words about the Christian life and the priorities of the church. It shouldn't be approached with the idea, "I need a hundred words in the next 45 minutes." Instead, you should spend time thinking about what subject the congregation most needs you to deal with, and how best to approach it. One good strategy is to have everything you're preparing to publish for the church reviewed by at least one other person whose communication skills you trust. Since most pastors don't do the whole newsletter, this idea could be used as well by whoever has responsibility for church publications.

Competent communication strives for clarity. I hope Mark doesn't beat himself up too much about his sermon mistake. What he can do is take it as a vivid reminder that clarity in communication is a constant struggle for ministers. He needs within a reasonable period of time to go back to those folk who misunderstood, and make sure that they have the chance to hear his heart. It's a mistake to assume that people will forget about it or get over it when we miscommunicate. At the very least, they often need reassurance that their feelings are important to us.

"College is spiritually dead" fiasco

Mark may also need to fine-tune his method of sermon preparation. The spontaneity and audience contact made possible by preaching without notes are powerful tools. The danger is precisely the difficulty Mark experienced. Pastors speaking without notes may not say what they think they are saying. At the very least, Mark should be open to the possibility of crafting sentences on sensitive topics so that he is absolutely sure he is saying what he means to say.

The same need for clarity is true in every arena in which a pastor communicates. Once during a tense deacons' meeting, I made a joke to relieve the tension. One deacon thought I was making light of the issue and took serious offense. In retrospect, it would have been better to save the humor for another time.

A pastor's primary tool is language. You can hear the echo of first-century church battles in the words of the apostle James:

> Not many of you should become teachers, my brothers and sisters, for you know that we who teach will be judged with greater strictness. For all of us make many mistakes. Anyone who makes no mistakes in speaking is perfect, able to keep the whole body in check with a bridle. If we put bits into the mouths of horses to make them obey us, we guide their whole bodies. Or look at ships: though they are so large that it takes strong winds to drive them, yet they are guided by a very small rudder wherever the will of the pilot directs. So also the tongue is a small member, yet it boasts of great exploits.
>
> How great a forest is set ablaze by a small fire! And the tongue is a fire.
>
> James 3:1-6a

Whatever happened to him, James passes along to us the damage the tongue can do, the difficulty of guarding what you say, and the necessity to do so. Every sermon, every conversation, every lesson, every article deserves our best thought, our careful preparation, and our constant effort to say what we mean.

Finally, competent communication requires listening. Since we pastors make our living by speaking, we often forget that others also have something to say. The truth, however, is that we can't know well what to say ourselves if we don't take the time and trouble to listen to others. You can preach a beautiful sermon, but if it doesn't speak to the needs of your congregation, your words are wasted.

You can know the decision you want a committee to make, but if you don't listen to others' ideas, you may miss the best course of action. You can offer counsel to a parishioner in trouble, but all good counselors remember that what people often want is not someone to solve their problems but rather someone to listen to their story and care about them in the listening. None of what I've said up to now in this chapter will do much good if the pastor who learns to write, speak, and otherwise communicate well doesn't also learn to listen.

How Do I Know if I'm Communicating Competently?

Obviously Mark wasn't communicating competently. He learned that from the phone calls. An irate phone call, however, is an exceedingly unpleasant way to secure the feedback we need about how well we are communicating. A better strategy is to search for ways to build multiple feedback loops into your ongoing relationship with the church.

A feedback committee. The United Methodist Church does a particularly good job with one facet of the kind of feedback I'm talking about. UMC congregations have as part of their standard committee structure a group called the pastor-parish relations committee. It is that committee's specific job to receive feedback from the congregation about the pastor's performance and to communicate that feedback to the pastor in appropriate ways. The goal is for the pastor to have the congregational input he or she needs to perform well.

Many denominations have something similar in their congregational structures, but by no means all. Often congregations limit themselves to a committee with administrative responsibility for supervising personnel. That is insufficient to be of real help because such committees tend to concentrate on job descriptions and performance reviews rather than on fostering communication between pastor and people. *[handwritten margin note: When & why is this necessary. Where is the crack in communication?]*

My recommendation is, if your church doesn't have a group whose specific responsibility is to give you feedback and support, start one. Tell your church board members that you need their help in doing the best job it's possible for you to do. Make sure that the committee is staffed with three to five of the most honest, discerning, and savvy members of the congregation. Then, meet with them regularly and listen.

A feedback session. Often pastors preach and lead without ever asking parishioners how they perceive what we are doing. One simple strategy is to hold a Sunday afternoon meeting from time to time for which the agenda is to receive feedback. These opinions can often be couched in the form of a responses to a particular sermon. Announce in advance that you're preaching on a topic that you want to discuss. It's important to give people permission to say what they think. Then provide a time and place for folk to come together and discuss what you've said. Have available a written outline or manuscript of your major points. Ask what they heard, and listen to the responses. Note that this is an important exercise *whether anyone comes to the session or not.* Providing a consistent opportunity for feedback creates an atmosphere in which people feel that their opinions are respected and heard even if they never bother to express them. Such a session may also provide the opportunity for feedback on items unrelated to the sermon itself. What's important is that you've given people a chance to tell you what they want to say.

Feedback sessions need not be limited to sermons. You can set up a session on virtually any question. For example, the question "How are we doing in our outreach to people in our community?" could become a fruitful topic for an afternoon coffee in the church parlor. The possibilities are endless.

A feedback form. An increasing number of churches provide a regular form that people can use to give feedback on a sermon or to send the minister a message. Such a form is sometimes put into the literature racks on the back of the pews or in the church foyer. One popular version is an "I Wish" pamphlet. The text consists of a number of unfinished sentences; for example, "I wish the pastor would preach about . . . ," "I wish a pastor would visit . . . ," or "I wish our church would address the issue of . . ." Specific items can be tailored for each congregation. Here again the benefits are twofold. You do get some feedback. And you create a culture in which people believe it is OK for them to give feedback.

Sometimes with regard to sermons it's helpful to structure a form that gives people an opportunity to provide feedback in a somewhat more formal fashion. The form at the end of the chapter, designed for the evaluation of student preachers, was adapted from one used at Western Theological Seminary, Holland, Michigan. Feel free to copy and adapt it for your setting. A form of this type, or one you create yourself, can prove invaluable as you work to become a more competent communicator.

The final word about feedback: "Never assume that you're communicating!"

> One friend reminds me we're always communicating something . . . but it may not be what we intend. JM

Always be eager to receive feedback and diligent about seeking it. Only by discovering what people are hearing can you adjust what and how you are communicating.

The real question with regard to Mark's preaching mistake is not so much whether he can avoid such mistakes in the future. All pastors make mistakes in communication. The real question is "Can Mark learn from his mistake, and can he communicate with those who misunderstood to minimize the damage and to keep his pastoral relationship with them in good repair?" Listening and caring will communicate more effectively than another sermon on the subject ever could. Good pastors practice competent communication!

Your Church Name

Evaluation of Preaching and Worship Leadership

Dear Member of the Congregation:

Thank you for completing this evaluation. The pastor will review your comments and suggestions, and this evaluation form will be shared with the Pastor/Parish Relations Committee. Your input will enable our minister to become more aware of strengths and weaknesses in the areas of preaching and worship leadership. Please be as specific as you can. Thank you.

Pastor/Parish Relations Committee

Date of Service: _____

Morning: _____   Evening: _____   (check one)

Name of Pastor: _____

Name of Evaluator (optional): _____

Church: _____

City: _____

Scripture: _____

Sermon Title: _____

1. GENERAL IMPRESSION
    a. The pastor's preaching was:
    Excellent ___ Very Good ___ Good___ Fair ___ Poor ___

    b. The pastor's leadership in worship was:
    Excellent ___ Very Good ___ Good___ Fair ___ Poor ___

    c. The pastor's reading of Scripture was:
    Excellent ___ Very Good ___ Good___ Fair ___ Poor ___

    d. Suggestions for improvement in preaching and/or worship leading:
    _____

    e. Things to continue because they were done well:
    _____

2. SERMON CONTENT
   a. How would you state the theme or basis idea of the sermon you have just heard?

   _____

   b. Please rate the following with a 'check' in the appropriate place.

   (1) How well did the sermon connect with the Scripture passage?

   No connection __|__|__|__|__|__|__|__|__|__ Close connection
                1 2 3 4 5 6 7 8 9 10

   (2) Did the sermon have practical application to your daily life?

   Irrelevant __|__|__|__|__|__|__|__|__|__ Relevant
            1 2 3 4 5 6 7 8 9 10

   (3) Was the content of the sermon easily understood?

   Confusing __|__|__|__|__|__|__|__|__|__ Clear
           1 2 3 4 5 6 7 8 9 10

   (4) Did the message move you in a positive direction in your Christian life?

   Unmoved __|__|__|__|__|__|__|__|__|__ Challenging
           1 2 3 4 5 6 7 8 9 10

3. SERMON DELIVERY
   a. Delivery was by: _____ reading a manuscript
                         _____ heavy dependence on notes
                         _____ few notes
                         _____ no notes
                         _____ well-delivered manuscript
   b. Evaluate the preacher's speaking ability in regard to:

   (1) Pulpit Presence

   Nervous __|__|__|__|__|__|__|__|__|__ Confident
           1 2 3 4 5 6 7 8 9 10

   (2) Eye Contact

   Poor __|__|__|__|__|__|__|__|__|__ Good
         1 2 3 4 5 6 7 8 9 10

   (3) Voice Projection

   Weak __|__|__|__|__|__|__|__|__|__ Strong
         1 2 3 4 5 6 7 8 9 10

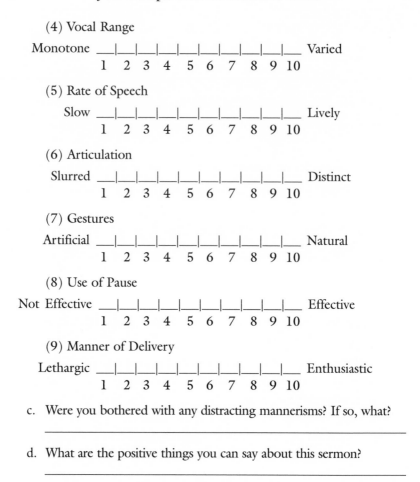

(4) Vocal Range

Monotone __|__|__|__|__|__|__|__|__|__ Varied
　　　　　　 1　2　3　4　5　6　7　8　9　10

(5) Rate of Speech

Slow __|__|__|__|__|__|__|__|__|__ Lively
　　　　 1　2　3　4　5　6　7　8　9　10

(6) Articulation

Slurred __|__|__|__|__|__|__|__|__|__ Distinct
　　　　　 1　2　3　4　5　6　7　8　9　10

(7) Gestures

Artificial __|__|__|__|__|__|__|__|__|__ Natural
　　　　　　 1　2　3　4　5　6　7　8　9　10

(8) Use of Pause

Not Effective __|__|__|__|__|__|__|__|__|__ Effective
　　　　　　　　 1　2　3　4　5　6　7　8　9　10

(9) Manner of Delivery

Lethargic __|__|__|__|__|__|__|__|__|__ Enthusiastic
　　　　　　 1　2　3　4　5　6　7　8　9　10

    c.　Were you bothered with any distracting mannerisms? If so, what?
_____

    d.　What are the positive things you can say about this sermon?
_____

Thank you for being honest and direct, and for the time and effort you have put into this evaluation. Your constructive criticism will help your pastor to be a more effective communicator of the gospel.

FOUR

A Time to Every Purpose

Competent Time Management

The fragrant smell from a dozen campfires filled the camp-ground. Eldon McIlroy, his wife, Beth, and their eight-year-old twins, Brittany and Brian, had strategically arranged themselves around their fireplace, deep in the family ritual of making s'mores. S'mores, as anyone who has ever been to camp could tell you, are that marvelous concoction of graham crackers, milk chocolate squares, and marshmallows that taste right only when the marshmallows are toasted over an open fire.

It was the third night of the McIlroys' annual two-week camping trip, and they hadn't yet really begun to relax. It had been a difficult spring at church. As a clergy couple in a 75/25 arrangement, Eldon and Beth usually coped fairly well with the demands of their parish and two rambunctious kids.

When the twins were born, Beth had cut back to quarter time to take the lead in child care. Eldon preached three Sundays out of four and did most of the administration. Beth used much of her time in pastoral care. With the occasional help of Eldon's parents as babysitters, they'd done pretty well.

This year had been a nightmare, though. Six deaths in January and February, an extensive remodeling project in Fellowship Hall, and all the extra work from a rules controversy in the denomination (not to mention Lent, Eastertide, Pente-cost, and T-ball) had left them both mentally and emotionally exhausted. John Frederickson at the next parish over had agreed to cover for emergencies, and the McIlroys had taken off without so much as a backward glance.

Suddenly Beth noticed that Eldon was staring down the row of campers. The park ranger's pickup was making its way slowly along toward their site. Beth's heart sank. "Mr. and Mrs. McIlroy?" the ranger asked, approaching apologetically. "Your congregation president has asked that you call her. There's been a death."

Half an hour later, Brian was still sniffling, and Brittany was comforting her doll while Eldon and Beth worked furiously to get the fold-down camper ready to start home. Sheila Johnson, the president of St. Mark's, had come home from work that evening to find her husband, John, dead in the driveway, apparently of a heart attack. Beth and Eldon were shocked and sad. They knew they had to go, but Beth was so angry about losing the vacation that she had a hard time even praying for Sheila. "We really needed this time off!" she muttered as she began arranging the back of the van. "The kids are so disappointed. Don't ministers ever really get away?"

The Issue: Competent Time Management

Managing your time as a minister just may be the single most difficult issue you face. The problem of managing ministerial time has a long and not very hopeful history. Until the Protestant Reformation, of course, priests were expected to give all their time to the work of ministry. With the rise of married clergy in Protestant life, the minister's family life quickly came to be seen as an important part of ministry. Beginning with Martin Luther's marriage to Katherine Van Bora, the minister and spouse were to serve as a model of the Christian family. A minister was expected to follow the biblical injunction and "manage his own household well" (1 Tim. 3:4). Keeping wife, children, and household life generally in good order came to be seen as a necessary demonstration of a minister's character.

The minister's need for Sabbath rest, time away from the job, and personal and family recreation was virtually ignored. Until the middle of the twentieth century, relatively little thought was given to ministers' need for a life apart from their work. At that point, a number of cultural factors came into play. The first was the general shortening of the work week as Americans moved off the farm and into business and industry. The rise of the American weekend and the increasing number of holidays and paid vacations advocated by the labor movement created an expectation of leisure in American life. In Christian circles the pastoral-care movement began to emphasize the need for ministers to be emotionally and physically healthy themselves in order to lead their congregations toward health. Increasingly, ministerial families balked at the notion that their personal lives should be absorbed into the life of the church. The women's movement taught women generally that it was unfair in any occupation to view women simply as appendages of their husbands. In many denominations, the increasing number of female ministers contributed to an important change in the dynamic of ministry. Over time women proved less willing than men to adopt a career-driven lifestyle to the detriment of their families. Growing numbers of men began to seek ways to balance their lifestyles. In my own earlier book on ministerial ethics I sought to construct a biblical rationale for ministerial time management.[1] Recognizing God's call to Christian vocation, I contended that Scripture supports rest and recreation for ministers just as it does for laypeople. These days few of us would fault Eldon and Beth for wanting a vacation free from congregational demands.

Counterbalancing these factors moving toward support for ministerial time off is the persistent cultural expectation that a minister should always be available to the congregation. Nobody would fault Sheila, the president of St. Mark's, for wanting her pastors with her at a time of devastating grief. Nor does anybody fault a church board for wanting the pastor present when important decisions are made. Nor does anyone fault the homebound for wanting the pastor to visit regularly. Nor does anyone deny that the pastor needs to socialize regularly with members of the church. Nor can one blame a family in crisis for wanting the pastor present in a time of need. The issue of ministerial time management grows out of this inevitable tension between the legitimate demands of congregational life and the legitimate need of ministers for a healthy and balanced lifestyle. As one of our senior students wrote in his self-assessment:

I think my last job as a worker in a feedlot prepared me for some of the demands of ministry. I believe working in a feedlot is much like being a pastor. It, too, was a seven-day-a-week job and the work was never done; I often got kicked and even run over a couple of times. There were many times when I'd have to go to work in the middle of the night to load or unload cattle and many times had to stay after supper to treat a pen of sick cattle. I slowly learned there will always be tomorrow, and if there isn't, it won't be my problem.[2]

I contend that time management is best addressed sequentially. By that I mean that a series of touch points punctuate a minister's relationship with a congregation—times when mutual expectations and intentions can be shaped and spelled out. Those touch points include the negotiation of an initial contract; the establishment of a ministerial schedule; the observation of contractual vacations, holidays and sabbaticals; the minister's daily self-management; and times of congregational change. For the most part, it is the skill with which we ministers address the issue at these critical points that determines whether people see us as competent time managers.

Negotiating a Contract

The problem of how you're going to manage your time as a pastor begins before you ever enter the parish. Most churches don't think of themselves as "hiring" a pastor. They think of themselves as "calling" one. And they assume that serving as their pastor will be the consuming passion of your life. They're correct. But that doesn't mean they have a right to your attention 168 hours a week.

Many churches, of course, can't afford a full-time pastor. Those congregations tend to prioritize the functions they want a pastor to perform and to set out the number of hours they believe they can reasonably expect for the money they pay. For example, it's not uncommon to see a small church hire a pastor for 20 hours per week. Those 20 hours might include Sunday morning, Wednesday evening, some visitation, and the necessary preparation time for worship. Difficulties arise only when a congregation expects more than can possibly be done in the allotted time or when the minister chooses to overfunction, working more hours than the contract states. In the first case, the congregation is chronically dissatisfied. In the second, the minister may be dissatisfied, or everybody may be happy until the next minister comes along and chooses *not* to overfunction.

When a congregation calls a minister full time, however, an entirely different set of expectations kicks in. These expectations come from a variety of sources: the local culture, the denominational tradition, the professions of the lay leadership, the performance of the previous minister, the work habits of existing staff, and the traditions of the congregation. The difficulty is that congregations are notoriously reluctant to spell out their expectations for a minister's work week. The dominant ethic seems to be something like: "We expect her to know what she needs to do and to spend the time it takes to do it." At first glance it sounds as though this kind of attitude gives the minister a great deal of freedom. In reality, it can lead to a quagmire of unfulfilled hopes and a sour relationship.

It's important to remember that there is a difference between a pastor's employment contract and her covenant with her people. A contract states the terms of employment and should be spelled out in detail. The covenant represents the mutual expectation that the pastor will provide a compassionate presence as God's representative in the community, whether the particular circumstance falls within her contract or not. JAH

The best initial defense against this kind of problem is to insist upon a written job description that includes a specified number of hours or days as the definition of a normal work week. Search committees may be reluctant to define your hours, but it's essential to get an understanding of your mutual expectations at the outset of your relationship.

Anticipating a full-time pastorate, you need first of all to define what is meant by full time. For example, though it has been fluctuating in recent years, the normal expectation for an hourly worker in America is still held to be 40 hours per week. Often it's assumed that "professionals"—doctors, lawyers, professors, business executives—may work 50 hours or more. It's not unusual to find pastors who work 60 hours or even more. George Barna, in his book *Turnaround Churches*, describes pastors who feel they may need to work 60 to 70 hours per week to help a declining church begin to grow again.[3] Think of the week as pastoral care expert Wayne Oates does in *The Minister's Own Mental Health*.[4] Oates divides the week into 21 periods—morning, afternoon, and evening for each of the seven days. In a typical 9-to-5, 40-hour job, work would consume 10 of the 21 periods. Acknowledging that pastors often work when others don't, Oates suggests that the rule of thumb for a pastor's normal week would be to work no more than 13 of the 21 periods. Put another way, that works out to a maximum of about 50 hours per week. There will always be crises, of course, but I believe that working more than 50 hours a week for sustained periods of time is dangerous to a minister's personal health, job performance, and family life.

Among its other effects, fatigue makes us vulnerable to bad judgment. For example, as a determined homebody, I rarely hang around and talk for long periods of time after meetings. In one church I served, the previous pastor had crossed boundaries with a female deacon. After I'd been in the church for a few months, one deacon

Employment expectations may vary widely depending upon the culture of the church. The pastor, for example, is often the only person a blue-collar worker has ever hired or been responsible for supervising. Lawyers think in terms of billable hours. Accountants tend to focus on the bottom line. Whatever their place in life, your people will tend to project their own employment experiences onto their relationship with you. JAH

observed, "I'm glad you go home when we're finished. X was always hanging around talking with Y after deacons' meeting. I'm sure that's how the trouble started." Clergy who cross boundaries do so in part when the church becomes their life instead of an appropriate part of their life.

The important consideration at this point is that some agreement be reached on what constitutes a normal work week in this job in this parish. In addition to defining a normal week, initial negotiations should also clarify policies for days off, vacations, sabbaticals, periodic holidays, and professional or study leave.

Enough vacation time is important. After seven years in one parish, I had worked my way up to four weeks' vacation. The next congregation, full of engineers for a local firm who were used to getting only two weeks, didn't like my proposal at all. I chose to accommodate to their culture, but quickly found that it was both a family and a personal mistake to have done so. I need three weeks in a block to unwind fully and genuinely get ready to go back to work. My family had grown to expect four weeks in a year as normal for us. The change created a barrier in our relationship with that church.

Many churches will grant extended time away as extra compensation for longer service. In one church I served, I got an extra month off in every fourth year. Another granted an extra two months after seven years of service. Whatever the details, sabbatical leave can be a powerful source of motivation for the minister, as well as providing opportunity for continuing education or extended rest. The time to secure such a benefit, however, is in your initial negotiation. Search committees will often want to put off the discussion of such a matter until later. From the minister's point of view, you are always in a much weaker negotiating position once you have agreed to come.

By "periodic holidays," I refer to a reality in ministerial life that is often overlooked. Ordinary Americans in recent decades have enjoyed the creation of several three-day weekends connected with federal holidays. These weekends, scattered throughout the year, give most families the opportunity for short trips or home projects or a break in the routine. Ministerial families never get these weekends. I recommend that you negotiate for at least four long weekends for your family during the course of the year in addition to your vacation. One suggestion is to make the 13th Sunday in each quarter of the year a regular day off for the preacher. It's important in the ministry to give your family as normal a life as possible. Taking a regular long weekend is one simple way to help.

> Ministerial children can be quite ingenious in communicating when they feel neglected. One southern pastor's son I heard about pulled the plug on the church's baptismal pool just before a scheduled service. When there was no water to perform the baptism, he got his father's attention. JAH

A final time category should be included in your initial contract—professional leave. Many churches grant a minister a week or two a year that can be used either for continuing education or for speaking engagements or other professional work outside the church. Again, if you plan to do this kind of thing, the terms and limits need to be spelled out in advance.

Once you have agreed with the search committee on the terms of your contract regarding time, it is equally important that the congregation discuss and approve these terms as part of their approval of your candidacy. If nothing else, when the subject comes up, you need to be able to say, "We settled all this before I came. I get four weeks vacation."

Establishing Your Weekly Schedule

The early months of a ministerial assignment constitute the second critical touch point in competent time management. The cliché "begin as you mean to go on" is the key operative phrase. Many ministers, overwhelmed by the need to get organized, to meet the parish, and to get off to a strong start, begin their work in a new congregation without regard to schedules, days off, and the need for study and preparation time. This, I believe, is a serious mistake.

The first piece in this particular puzzle is to establish your day off. Most ministers, in addition to as much of Saturday as they can get, take one other day off in the week as a Sabbath, which most people take on Sunday. Two primary theories seem to operate here. Some ministers take Monday to recover from the rigors of Sunday. Some take Friday to create at least the possibility of a normal weekend. I tried both and found that taking Monday off to recover did not work well for me. I didn't like feeling that bad on my own time! In addition, some argue that Saturday is never satisfactory. At a minimum, you're always subconsciously preparing for Sunday.

The day you take, of course, is not as important as that you take it and take it seriously. The biblical pattern of Sabbath rest needs to inform us here. The Hebrews believed it so important to observe the law that they took great pains to define what was work and what was not. Obviously occasions arise when a pastor needs to work on a day off. When there is a death or a crisis, most pastors expect to be there. But not every phone call is a crisis. Not every theological question necessarily requires an answer today. A church member's imminent death would, for most of us, be a sufficient cause for coming in to work. A youth-group kid's breaking a leg would not for many of us be sufficient reason to interrupt the family trip to the mall, especially if someone else was designated as congregational caregiver for the day.

It's important that the pastor have an understanding with the church secretary (if there is one) and the chair of the church board as to what constitutes a legitimate reason for interrupting a day off. These two individuals can do a great deal to make a day-off policy work. By fielding calls or visits to the church office, the secretary can say, for example, "I'm sorry—Pastor Larry is gone for the day, but Deacon Mary Jones would be happy to come and sit while you have your boil lanced." The chair of the church board can help keep the day clear of meetings and other calendared events. The pastor, of course, should also be ready to say, "I'm sorry but that's my day out of the office. Can the flower committee meet without me?" The day can also be communicated in other ways, such as a notation wherever the church calendar is published. Most church members will want to respect and support their pastor's time away once they know about it. For example, with regard to family supper time, I've normally told congregations that we don't answer the phone during supper. That's our daily time for connecting as a family. Nobody ever grumbled. They just called back later or left a message.

In a multiple-pastor staff, it seems likely that people should take off different days (for example, one on Monday, one on Friday). In fact, that limits greatly the amount of time one has with one's colleagues. In several congregations I've served, all the pastors took the same day off (usually Friday). JM

With your day off in place, the rest of your work week needs to be divided in ways that allow you to get your work done. Many pastors begin their workday with prayer. This time is seen as an important part of their work and should be protected from interruption by everyday events such as phone calls. A competent secretary will learn to field requests with such phrases as "He's at prayer now. He'll be finished in half an hour. Do I need to interrupt him?"

A similar strategy works for study time and sermon-preparation time. In every church I served, I taught the people that Thursday was the day I wrote my sermon. They learned not to call on that day unless it was important, and for those who were unaware of the day, my secretaries became adept at learning when, and when not, to interrupt me. Some in the congregation would tell me they always remembered me in prayer that morning. Others would jokingly suggest that they'd try never to have a crisis on Thursday because a good sermon was too important.

For anyone serving a larger church or a rural church, it's also important to have a strategy for hospital visitation. Larger churches may have a number of individuals hospitalized at one time. In rural churches it may be necessary to drive considerable distances to visit those hospitalized. The specifics of such a strategy will vary according to congregational expectations, local custom, and the severity of the illness. Some churches expect the pastor to visit every day the patient is hospitalized. Others expect one visit, with subsequent visits only if the stay is extended. When the illness is life-threatening, most families expect daily contact. Early in the pastor's tenure, it's important to discover what local custom has been and to build time into one's schedule to accommodate the need.

For pastors with young families, especially, the issue of evening responsibilities has to be addressed. In the tradition from which I come, Sunday and Wednesday evening worship services were usual. Visitation was conducted on Tuesday evenings, and Monday was the normal evening for committees to meet. That meant it was not unusual for me to be out of the home four evenings a week. I worked very hard in the churches I served to shift committee meetings to Sunday evenings and Wednesday evenings after worship and to take care of as much visiting as possible during the day. For pastors with school-age children, weekday evenings are critical times for helping with homework and with routine matters such as bedtime. Pastors cannot maintain adequate involvement in their family life when they are gone more than half the evenings in the week.

Many pastors, of course, will try to handle this problem by shifting primary parenting responsibility to the other parent. I believe that this kind of abdication of parental involvement because "Daddy is the pastor" or "Mommy has more important things to do" is both unbiblical and wrong. It is wrong because of the clear demonstration of psychological data that children need the involvement of both parents for balanced development. The history of the Protestant churches is littered with anecdotes of preacher's kids who turned out badly in part because their ministerial parent was never around. Abdicating parental involvement is unbiblical because the institution of the family was created before the church and must take precedence over it.

↑ Taking Your Time

Once you've established a "normal" routine for you, with a schedule of work and rest that enables you both to get your work done and to stay strong for the journey, the trick is sticking with it. I treat this matter as a separate section because many of us have excellent contracts. We simply fail to observe them.

Eldon and Beth in our opening story face the classic pastoral dilemma. How do you choose between two legitimate needs, one urgent and the other equally important? First, at times the nature of the crisis is such that you simply have to go home. In 2004 Hurricane Charley devastated a large portion of west central Florida. Imagine a pastor from the town of Punta Gorda who happened to be on vacation in New York when the hurricane came through. She would want to be home as soon as it was possible to get there. Failing to go home in such a circumstance would be a serious breach of pastoral responsibility.

Beyond such clear crises, however, lies a large grey area where it's more difficult to decide. There's no perfect answer to the problem of when to go home, but some helps are available that you can put into practice. In some denominations it is customary for a neighboring pastor to agree to take pastoral-care responsibility while you are gone. If you don't have such a custom in your area, it might be possible over time to put an exchange of caregiving into practice.

If you're in a multi-staff situation, other ministers in your own local church can cover for you. The degree to which you are comfortable with that will depend upon the nature of your relationship and of their responsibilities and training. In a small church, lay leaders can be trained to give pastoral care. Again, the degree to which you are comfortable with their work will depend largely upon the individual.

I described Eldon and Beth's scenario to one pastor friend who said with a laugh, "The problem is they camped too close to home!" He had a point. One way to get beyond the possibility of being called home is to go to a place where the cost or the timing of changing your plans is prohibitive. If they have to, your parishioners really can get by without you.

What happens to most pastors with regard to days off and periodic holidays is more insidious than the scenario of a crisis while you're on vacation. It's the kind of creeping erosion of your time off that occurs when you agree to do first one thing, then another and another, at times you're scheduled to be away. As a pastor I found that there was always worthwhile church work that needed doing on my day off, no matter what day I chose.

What is required for competence here is the kind of mental toughness that recognizes that none of us is indispensable to the kingdom of God, but each of us is indispensable to our family and to our own mental, physical, spiritual, and emotional well-being. The ecumenical hunger committee will go ahead and meet even if you're not there. Your relationship with the church member who invites you to lunch on your day off will survive if you decline the invitation. But your child may never forget that you canceled a trip to the zoo to meet with the church's architect. In short, you need to take your day off. You need to take it weekly. And when you don't get to take it, for unavoidable reasons, you need to make it up. To fail to do so is to ignore the wisdom of Sabbath.

For many ministers the question of taking a contractual sabbatical raises the level of tension considerably. Most ministers feel a keen sense of responsibility for the well-being of the congregation. The idea of an extended absence for any reason goes against the grain. Being gone for yourself for an extended period of time, even when the time away is badly needed, feels especially selfish. Moreover, regardless of what they may have agreed to when they hired you, some church members will begin to complain whenever you're gone for more than two weeks at a time.

One key strategy here is to include the congregation well in advance in your preparations to be away. As you begin planning, thank the members from the pulpit for their maturity and wise foresight in providing sabbatical rest for their pastors. Tell them what you intend to do, and why it will be beneficial. Help them to feel that they are participants in the process of providing this time away. Assign as many of your pastoral tasks as possible to committees and individuals in the congregation. Let them know you're counting on them to fill in while you're gone and looking for good reports on what they've accomplished when you return. Help them to see this occasion as their chance both to understand better what you do and to develop their own skills and confidence in ministry. The more the congregation sees your sabbatical as something that reaps benefits for the members both in their own growth and in your well-being and energy when you return, the easier your time away will be.

It's also important to recognize what's reasonable when you set up a sabbatical plan. Too long an absence can damage the legitimate emotional ties that bind a pastor and congregation together. I followed one pastor who took maximum advantage of the church's sabbatical policy during his tenure. He would be gone for three months at a time. Whether their feelings were healthy or not, the church members came to resent his time away and to feel that it was excessive. I cut my block of time away to two months and found the church to be more accepting and cooperative. Roy Oswald, in his excellent book on clergy self-care, argues for a three-month time frame.[5] The point here is to suit your practice to your context.

Managing the Day

At best, sabbaticals and vacations are a rare occurrence. For many of us, the most serious challenge in competent time management is neither finding a block of time to take a sabbatical nor making the effort to create a healthy daily schedule on paper. The most serious challenge is adhering to the schedule we say we have.

The first element in competent daily self-management is knowing and meeting your own needs for adequate exercise and rest. An increasing body of medical research is showing that adults need eight to nine hours of sleep to function well. Doctors are virtually unanimous that we all need a minimum of 30 minutes' exercise every day. If we fail in these two simple aspects of self-care, we will damage our effectiveness in virtually every area of our lives. I tend to be an early-to-bed, early-to-rise person. It's relatively easy for me to get to bed and then get up, exercise, and get to work in the morning.

That may not work for you. You may like to stay up late and hate any activity before 11 a.m. If your natural rhythm is to be a night owl, look for ways to organize your time to make maximum use of your evenings. For example, you may be a person who should do your daily devotional reading and prayer at night rather than subjecting God to your grumpiness in the morning. You might even combine exercise and devotion. I knew one seminary professor, who happened to be deaf, who would turn off his hearing aids and walk three miles from his home to and from campus every day. He accomplished prayer, exercise, and his daily commute all at the same time. At a minimum, in the context of your own tradition's practices, it's essential to build in time for your own personal relationship with God.

I swim regularly. As I do, I focus on the pennants above the pool, one at a time. Each one represents a person or concern (or the congregation itself) for whom I pray. This practice is also helpful in my letting go of the tensions and stresses of my work. JM

The very nature of pastoral life works against keeping a schedule. The phone is always ringing. Someone is dropping in. Sudden crises or opportunities can interrupt the day. It's frighteningly easy to get to the end of a day without having accomplished anything you intended to do.

For me the simple technique of making a list helped greatly. During my devotional time each morning, I would jot down those items that I believed needed attention during the day. As each was attended to, I crossed it off the list. At the end of the day, I carried over unfinished items to the next day's list. The process gave me a sense of accomplishment and helped alleviate that feeling of "never being finished" which often plagues the pastoral life. Simple techniques from the business world can also be helpful. *The One Minute Manager,* for example, offers a number of ideas that can be adapted to the administrative areas of ministerial life.[6]

A veteran pastor stopped at my office door one day and asked how things were going. I lamented that I wasn't getting anything done because there'd been so many interruptions. "Ministry *is* interruptions," he said. While I like to accomplish those tasks on my list every day, I think he is correct. Part of feeling satisfied in our work is coming to terms with its unpredictability and not fighting that reality. That does not mean we have no boundaries! JM

Even with the best of management, of course, a day or a week will often get away from you. There's no way to plan for the week when three homebound seniors die within 36 hours. One key to responsible time management on a continuing basis comes from Oates's insight about managing the time blocks in your week (see page 64). He recommends that you typically work no more than 13 units per week. If circumstances require you to work 15 of the 21 units in a given week, why not take off an extra two units the next week to keep your average at 13? Approaching your work week with this kind of sliding scale both allows the necessary flexibility to deal with situations as they arise and keeps in mind the goal of adequate rest, recreation, and time with family and friends. Somebody, sometime, has to mow the lawn, do the laundry, clean the house, and buy the groceries!

If you're having trouble getting your schedule under control with Oates's time blocks, you might find it helpful to look at your time use in smaller increments. For example, take a two-week period and keep track of

In my experience pastors of multi-staff congregations can help legitimize the concept of "compensatory time off" by insisting that staff members take such time. The pastor should be willing to say to a church leader, "Kristy is not in the office today. She put in many extra hours last week, so I told her to take the day off and get some rest." When pastors protect staff members in this manner, they create a work environment in which they also find it easier to do as suggested here. MAS

every 15 minutes of your time at work. Then take a hard look at how you used that time. Did you spend excess time talking with others in the office, surfing the Net, or playing with PowerPoint? How could you discipline yourself to free up more time for productive work?

Managing Change

Ordinary church life moves along according to a yearly rhythm of the seasons. Both the secular year and the Christian year come into play. Advent is always busy. Summertime may be eerily quiet. Most ministers learn to manage these seasonal fluctuations quite well. More stressful and more difficult, though, are the times when significant changes in your routine or the church's are in the offing. Such times include the first and last six months of a pastorate, any kind of major mobilization of the congregation such as a revival, a capital funding or building campaign, or any time the community or the nation as a whole is in the midst of crisis. During these times it's important for ministers to respond in a way that offers stability and encouragement to the congregation. There is no magic formula here, but some basic insights can serve as a guide.

First, even in times of great change, life still goes on. People are born and baptized; they marry and die. Sunday worship happens every seven days. A competent minister pays attention to the daily and weekly details of life—even when the world seems to be crashing in around you.

The rationale for this dogged attention to detail is simple. In times of crisis we need to be pointed back again and again to the God-given order of our days. In a world where nothing seems reliable anymore, *you* can be dependable, and by that very stability you witness to the dependability of God. Even as you come to the end of your ministry in a church, your continued attention to detail will reassure the congregation that life will go on when you are gone. You may be leaving in August, but if you normally convene the committee to work on the annual October stewardship emphasis in June, go ahead and call the meeting. Churches know that ministers come and go and that the work of the church ultimately is theirs. What they need as you go is your blessing on that process. It's important that you not be so eager to "get the heck out of Dodge" that you forget their lives will go on even when you've moved to the promised land of First Church, Nexttown.

A second principle of your time management in times of change concerns blessing your members to specific ministry tasks. We ministers tend to be control freaks. We like to run the capital campaign ourselves, "so that it's done right." We really don't believe that anyone else will be as picky as we are with the contractor building the new sanctuary. We believe we'll do the best job of matching talent and committee responsibilities for the coming year. As a result we spend way too much of our time doing things that other people could perfectly well do, and, even more damaging, we communicate that we really don't trust the congregation to be competent. When you consciously step back from a task and tell someone else that you believe he or she can do it, you give a blessing that is surprisingly rare in modern life.

In the funny little book *The Penguin Principles,* two experienced Lutheran pastors advise ministers to adopt a kind of "creative ignorance" when it comes to the daily work of the church.[7] Their argument is that we ministers do too much for our congregations that they could just as easily do for themselves. In fact the lay members need to work without us for the benefit of their own self-esteem and growth as disciples.

In times of stress it's especially difficult for us to bless others' work. When we're stressed ourselves, it's harder for us to trust others. But I believe it's precisely in these times that people can and will experience their most significant service and growth as disciples, if we give them the chance to do it.

The third principle of time management in crisis times seems at first glance to contradict the other two, but it doesn't. Our first principle seems to be task-oriented. The second seems to back off from specific involvement in solving problems. I place this one third because adhering to the first two principles will help make following this one possible. In times of crisis, people need ministry to be relatively "high-touch." In other words, they need you to keep in contact, stay close, and let them know that you care. By paying attention to the ordinary routines of ministry and by empowering the laity to solve the crisis, you gain the time and energy to invest in caring for people.

It's a truism of crisis ministry that what you say when you meet the family at the hospital after the accident does not much matter. What matters is that you're there. When you're getting ready to leave the church, people need time to say good-bye. They will each do that in their own way, at their own pace. Some will do it at the church's formal farewell, and that will be plenty for them. Others will need to drop by your office. The same kinds of personal variations hold true when the church is engaged in a big project. Some need your encouragement to meet whatever responsibility they've accepted. Some need to voice their opposition. Some just need to hear you say, "Well done." Similarly, when the church is in conflict, it's crucial that you stay in touch with all parties, especially those you believe to be most alienated. The wheels of change are lubricated by the quality of relationships in a congregation, and the pastor is a crucial actor in keeping those relationships healthy. When the church is in the midst of change, concentrate your time and energy in pastoral care.

This Test Is Worth the Time!

Good managers of time tend to know that they do well with scheduling. And poor time managers tend to know how badly they do. But if you're not sure how well you're doing, here's a brief quiz to help you think about your time-management skills. Mark the following statements true or false for you. The more you answer with "false," the more your time-management skills need a tune-up.

1. My sermon is always substantially finished before Saturday. T F
2. I am rarely, if ever, late for meetings. T F
3. I visit members, those in nursing homes and those who are homebound, on a regular schedule. T F
4. I take my day off weekly, except for genuine emergencies. T F
5. I have a regular daily time for devotion and prayer. T F
6. My secretary knows the day I prepare my sermon. T F
7. I think that I spend most of my time on the most important things. T F
8. I'm confident that I visit hospital patients often enough during their stay. T F
9. I almost always attend my children's school and sports events. T F
10. Our family takes at least two weeks' vacation every year. T F
11. I seem to have enough time for myself. T F
12. My sermons are usually planned several weeks in advance. T F
13. I sleep eight hours a night. T F
14. I exercise half an hour or more several days a week. T F
15. My spouse and I set aside time to be with each other. T F
16. Church people feel that I'm accessible. T F
17. I am home four or more evenings per week. T F
18. My desk top is cleaned regularly. T F
19. I list the tasks I hope to accomplish each day. T F
20. I get adequate time each week for study and prayer. T F
21. I try never to do things someone else could do just as well. T F

Time management is not an exact science. Nor is it the same for each person. But good time management can make the difference between a successful, fulfilling ministry, and one that seems to splash about aimlessly in the shallows. Most important, time management is a skill that can be learned, and learning it is worth the time!

For Further Reading

Competence in time management can be enhanced in a number of ways. The following works approach the subject from different angles:

The author draws heavily on pastoral-care and business models to fashion a time-management strategy. Farm life provides a third model. On a family farm, tasks may be divided into daily, weekly, seasonal, and emergency categories. Planning and timely work make for success. Farming life includes numerous "down times" as well: bad weather, post-harvest, and the like. Wise farmers accept and enjoy such times of refreshment. Farmers, like ministers, may thrive, provided they take advantage of the natural rhythms associated with their work. MAS

Barna, George. *Turnaround Churches.* Ventura, Calif.: Regal Books, 1993.
Blanchard, Kenneth, and Spencer Johnson. *The One Minute Manager.* New York: Berkley Books, 1981.
Covey, Stephen R. *The Seven Habits of Highly Effective People: Restoring the Character Ethic.* New York: Simon & Schuster, 1989.
Oswald, Roy M. *Clergy Self-Care: Finding a Balance for Effective Ministry.* Herndon, Va.: Alban Institute, 1991.

FIVE

My Yoke Is Easy

Competent Stress Management

"Ouch!" Joan Lindstrom hobbled painfully to her car. It was happening again—stress-related eczema. From the time she was a little girl, Joan had been subject to periodic bouts of painful blisters on her feet. During her childhood the doctor assumed it was athlete's foot. As a college student Joan herself had realized that the attacks came in periods of high stress. Just after exams she could count on limping for a week.

Now, after wrangling with the church finance committee for nearly a month over next year's budget proposal, Joan knew exactly what was causing this latest flare-up. The more she dealt with intractable, frustrating situations, the more subject she was to physical symptoms.

And this year's budget debate was a corker. The closing of a local technology plant had cost the church five tithing families in the past six months. The fellowship was healthy, and everybody knew they would recover eventually. But that didn't help the short-term income projections. Joan was urging the committee to have faith and to focus on the church's ministry vision, but a slim majority of fiscal conservatives on the committee were determined to cut programs drastically.

Joan felt her body sag wearily into the car seat. "I hate feeling this way!" she told herself as she pulled onto the street on her way home. "I'm tense; I'm not sleeping; I'm irritable with the family. I've got to learn to manage this kind of thing better, or I'm really going to get sick!"

79

Distracted, driving with half her mind as she fretted over the meeting she'd just come from, Joan failed to notice the car braking suddenly just ahead of her. Abruptly her sense of danger kicked in. She hit her brake, checking her momentum, but failed to keep herself from sliding into the Chevy ahead as its driver waited for a confused dog to get out of the road. Wham! Fortunately her seat belt held. "Oh, no!" Joan wailed to herself as she got out shakily to inspect the damage. "Whatever is Jim going to say?"

The Issue: Managing Stress

Everybody has stress. Every job is stressful. "Stress," pastoral counselor Wayne Oates observes, "is like the heat in your body or in the engine of your automobile."[1] Some stress is necessary to life itself. Without the stress of digestion and circulation, your body can't live. Without the stress of combustion your car can't go. So some stress is good.

Any minister knows, however, that stress can accumulate to the point of doing damage. Many of us may not be as lucky as Joan in our opening vignette. Her body tells her when she's dealing with too much stress. She has a clear and painful incentive to take better care of herself. We may not have such an obvious physical symptom when we are overstressed. Still, the consequences of too much stress for any of us are real and sometimes downright dangerous.

This is not an "academic" issue for me. At age 31 I was completing my third year of marriage, working toward my doctoral prelims, and serving in my first pastorate in a small rural church. The church was a powder keg as the result of an affair between two leaders whom I had confronted that summer. One night my wife and I stayed in the city, so that I could take my exams early the next morning. The church knew we'd be away, and our parsonage was broken into and our gold jewelry stolen—the charm bracelet for which she'd been accumulating charms since she was a child, along with our high school and college rings. The next month I was diagnosed with Type 1 diabetes. Stress had triggered my genetic predisposition to the disease.

> Women often fall victim to the "silent killer" of heart disease because sometimes there are no apparent symptoms. JM

Diabetes, heart disease, obesity, hypertension, and a host of other physical conditions can be directly or indirectly related to stress. In addition, its consequences are often felt in our relationships, our family life, our performance at work, and our general sense of well-being.

For ministers, of course, the issue is not how to get rid of stress. That simply isn't possible. The issue is how to manage the inevitable stresses of our profession in such a way that we actually experience for ourselves the "abundant life" Christ promised his followers, rather than merely calling others to that experience. The senior ministerial students from my seminary's Readiness for Ministry colloquium tend to address this issue of stress management in terms of their own typical coping mechanisms. They may say, for example, "I try to deal with stress by being flexible" or "I have to know in myself when to walk away." Coping mechanisms are indeed important. Perhaps even more crucial, though, is learning to recognize how stress accumulates in our lives and how to optimize our stress management on a daily basis.

One of the key researchers in the area of stress was Hans Selye. See, for example, his book *Stress Without Distress* (New York: New American Library, 1975). Selye distinguishes between stress, distress, and eustress. All of life is stressful. Sometimes it's painful, and that's distress. Sometimes it's enjoyable, and that's eustress. Too much stress of any kind can interfere with our ability to cope. Selye identified the General Adaption Syndrome (GAS) as our response to stress. With too much stress, we run out of GAS! Although the process of adaption is the same, we all have different ways of responding to the stressors in our lives. JAH

Recognizing Stress

Traditional explanations of stress describe it as a threefold process. It begins with alarm. Our equilibrium is threatened by some challenge. This challenge can be as simple as getting through the day at work or as devastating as a diagnosis of cancer. A pastor may have to meet with the finance committee, preach on a controversial issue, or deal with the death of a well-loved member. As soon as the challenge begins, stress begins. The second phase is our effort to restore our equilibrium. The runner seeks to make it to the finish line to rest. The person who has just been fired gets angry to protect his or her self-esteem. The pastor looks for a way to make a disgruntled member happy. The third phase is ③ exhaustion. We've done all we can do. If the challenge does not go away, the stress continues. If we have successfully met it, the stress is alleviated, though we will still need to rest.

Stress also has a cumulative effect, however. The more stressful events one deals with in a given period of time, the more likely one's body is to react negatively. Almost 40 years ago significant research created a stress scale as a way of assigning weight to this cumulative effect of stress in our lives. That scale was later adapted by Roy Oswald for the specific stresses faced by ministers.[2] Oswald's scale follows:

Triggers for Stress

Rank	Life Event	Mean Value
1	Death of a spouse	100
2	Divorce	73
3	Marital separation	65
4	Death of a close family member	63
5	Personal injury or illness	53
6	Marriage	50
7	Serious decline in church attendance	49
8	Geographical relocation	49
9	Private meetings by segment of congregation to discuss your resignation	47
10	Beginning of heavy drinking by immediate family member	46
11	Marital reconciliation	45
12	Retirement	45
13	Change in health of family member	44
14	Problem with children	42
15	Pregnancy	40
16	Sex difficulties	39
17	Alienation from one's board/council/session/vestry	39
18	Gain of new family member	39
19	New job in new line of work	38
20	Change in financial state	38
21	Death of close friend	37
22	Increased arguing with spouse	35
23	Merger of two or more congregations	35

24	Serious parish financial difficulty	32
25	Mortgage over $50,000 (home)	31
26	Difficulty with member of church staff (associates, organist, choir director, secretary, janitor)	31
27	Foreclosure of mortgage or loan	30
28	Destruction of church by fire	30
29	New job in same line of work	30
30	Son or daughter leaving home	29
31	Trouble with in-laws	29
32	Anger of influential church member over pastor action	29
33	Slow, steady decline in church attendance	29
34	Outstanding personal achievement	28
35	Introduction of new hymnal to worship service	28
36	Failure of church to make payroll	27
37	Remodeling or building program	27
38	Start or stop of spouse's employment	26
39	Holiday away	26
40	Start or finish of school	26
41	Death of peer	26
42	Offer of call to another parish	26
43	Change in living conditions	25
44	Revision of personal habits	24
45	Negative parish activity by former pastor	24
46	Difficulty with confirmation class	22
47	Change in residence	20
48	Change in schools	20
49	Change in recreation	19
50	Change in social activities	18
51	Death/moving away of good church leader	18
52	Mortgage or loan less than $50,000	17
53	Change in sleeping habits	16
54	Development of new friendship	16
55	Change in eating habits	15
56	Stressful continuing education experience	15
57	Major program change	15
58	Vacation at home	13
59	Christmas	12
60	Lent	12
61	Easter	12
62	Minor violations of the law	11

This scale does not, of course, provide for differences in age or gender. Losing a spouse, for example, is devastating at any age. But a 20-year-old may handle that grief very differently from a 75-year-old. Nor is the scale adjusted for inflation. The mortgage that cost $50,000 in 1982 was over $95,000 in 2003. Still the idea is valid. The scale offers a way to gauge the cumulative effect of stress in your life. Simply add up the mean value of the events that apply to you. The closer your score is to 250 points or above, the more likely you are to suffer an adverse change in health caused by stress. I've already mentioned my own genetic predisposition to diabetes. Many of us have similar "defects" in our genetic code that can become more likely to cause trouble when our body is affected by stress.

Note that I chose to provide you with this scale because it is the classic of its genre. Any number of scales have been developed since that time to measure a variety of stress-related conditions. A quick Internet search for "stress scale" will reveal many of these, often in the public domain and ready for downloading.

DEALING
w/ STRESS

The first key skill in competent management, then, is learning to ① *recognize the stressors* you face so that you can take steps to alleviate a crisis or to cope amid the ongoing pressures of life. Often we tend to deny the reality of stress involved in activities related to our work and family life. The statement "But I really enjoyed going to camp with 50 middle-schoolers!" may be true. But that doesn't lessen the stress involved in the situation. That long-awaited family vacation will get you away from the stress of work, but it will also create some significant stress of its own. As I write these pages, my own family consists of a seminary professor, an elementary school librarian, and a sixth-grader. We've just decided not to go camping this weekend because we're all three stressed out from starting the semester this week. The closer we got to the fun, the less we wanted the stress!

So how do you recognize the stress you're under in the church? Remember Paul?

> Are they ministers of Christ? I am talking like a madman—I am a better one: with far greater labors, far more imprisonments, with countless floggings, and often near death. Five times I have received from the Jews the forty lashes minus one. Three times I was

beaten with rods. Once I received a stoning. Three times I was shipwrecked; for a night and a day I was adrift at sea; on frequent journeys, in danger from rivers, danger from bandits, danger from my own people, danger from Gentiles, danger in the city, danger in the wilderness, danger at sea, danger from false brothers and sisters; in toil and hardship, through many a sleepless night, hungry and thirsty, often without food, cold and naked. And, besides other things, I am under daily pressure because of my anxiety for all the churches.

2 Corinthians 11:23-28

Notice how many of our prototypical pastor's experiences earn Paul significant points on our stress scale! And some others aren't even considered. Imagine how many points you'd get for being in a shipwreck! So, just for fun, let's say you and Paul are competing for first prize at a "pity party." How many stressors can you name from the past year? How many points do they earn you? Because many of us get so busy living our lives that we forget to evaluate the stress, it's a good policy three or four times a year to write down the stressors in your life and see how they add up. Counting your stressors is not really a matter of seeking pity, of course. It is a matter of gauging when you're overloaded and need to take action to care for yourself.

Managing Stress

Once you have recognized that you are under stress as a minister, the next step is to give yourself permission to manage it. This is not as simple as it sounds. Many of us ministers seem to feel that we are spiritually required to absorb whatever challenges come our way. From a biblical and theological standpoint, it's important to remember that in the earliest annals of the Hebrew people God provides periodic rest for God's people. It's called the Sabbath, and it's built into the structure of the week precisely because it's not good for us to work all the time. When we're dealing with the weekly stresses of life, a weekly Sabbath can go a long way toward restoring our equilibrium. Many of us ministers have gotten pretty good at counseling our people not to work all the time. Because of the nature of the ministerial job, however, too many of us seem to feel that we must be working or at least "on call" 24 hours a day, seven days a week. As a result, we never get the Sabbath rest we urge upon our people. Our stress accumulates without a respite.

In chapter 4 we talked about strategies for managing time, particularly the amount of time you will work in a given week. Those time-management skills are essential. But the "right to rest," as Oates describes it in another of his books, is part of the very structure of creation and redemption.[3] As finite creatures we are made to need rest. We are also given the gift of rest. As children of God through the grace of Christ, we are freed from the everlasting need to prove our own worth. When Jesus says, "Come to me, all you that are weary and are carrying heavy burdens, and I will give you rest" (Matt. 11:28), he is profoundly restructuring human existence, releasing us to participate in a life of grace.

So to manage stress, it is critical to accept your right to a Sabbath as a child of God. And the only way to experience your right of Sabbath is to take one regularly. Regular rest helps calm our spirits, gives our bodies a chance to rejuvenate, provides opportunity for a change of scene, and allows us to pursue recreational activities we cannot do when we're "on call." If you're not getting at least one full day away from the job every week, you've missed an important part of God's gift of rest for us. I won't recapitulate here the time-management strategies mentioned in an earlier chapter. But I will say, "Use them!"

In addition, develop a theology that sees this regular time of rest as a gift of God in our lives that must be honored. One friend of mine has cultivated Sabbath in her life by simply saying, when appropriate, "I don't work on Sunday." Think how freeing it would be to have one day in your week when your answer to the "emergency" committee meeting, or to the request for a "more convenient" time for counsel-

---

Healthy people will create strategies for dealing with stress. Here are some guidelines:

1. Develop a *number of alternative* actions for dealing with any given situation whether you like them or not.

2. *Recognize* and *accept* your own *strengths* and *limitations*.

3. Go through the *majority of your waking hours* feeling good about yourself.

4. Develop the biblical discipline of *agape*, defined as to will and to work for the well-being of others.

5. Create and cultivate a reliable community of faith. JAH

ing, or to your own compulsion to get that project done around the house, could be, "I'm sorry, but that day is my Sabbath."

A further strategy for managing stress involves maintaining a holistic perspective on the issue. Because we experience stress as physical, mental, spiritual, emotional, social/interpersonal, and vocational, the full range of strategies comes into play in stress management. Ministerial families, for example, often feel socially isolated. They may not feel entirely safe pursuing deep social relationships within the church family.

That means we have to find ways to build a supportive social life beyond our church. Some clergy are so drained spiritually by their duties that they need to find a regular place outside their own parish. Regular exercise, enough sleep, adequate nutrition, healthy personal relationships, good mental health, supportive professional relationships, and a vigorous spiritual life all come into play in giving us

> In stressful situations within the church it's important to identify your personal resources. Who is the pastor's pastor? Who is the pastor's family's pastor? JAH

the tools we need to cope with the stresses of life. Ministers who neglect these common-sense habits are like people who drive without a seatbelt. They may go on for a while without obvious damage, but they could be headed for eventual catastrophe.

Coping with Pressure

Beyond simple attention to good habits, most of us as ministers still need help in dealing with day-to-day pressures. The ministry is a job that is never completed. There is always one more visit that could be made, one more telephone call. Often ministers founder from the constant weight of all that needs to be done.

We must recognize that we will never get finished. In 20 years as a pastor I never once went home at the end of the day having completed everything that I could have done. For many of us this lack of closure in our work isn't a source of pressure. But many of us do feel that pressure to finish. To help alleviate the inevitable stress we feel as a result of that pressure, we can learn to rethink the way we approach our day.

For me that rethinking is at least initially theological. As Christians, we live our days in the presence of Christ. My first act when I get to the office is to pray for the events of the day. I ask the Lord to "redeem the time" (Eph. 5: 16 KJV), to be with me, to help me set my priorities, and to make me aware of opportunities that arise to bear witness or to be of help to others. As the last portion of my prayer for the day, I make a list of tasks to be addressed. Then I begin to work. Periodically during the day I renew my prayer. Not long before time to go home, I ask the Lord and myself if there's anything else that must be done immediately. If so, I do it. If not, I go home. Frequently I don't get through my whole list in a day. But I'm able to rest, because I feel that, with the Lord's help, I've used the day to best advantage.

Get comfortable in your pew; I'm going to preach for a moment here. The process I describe above is not merely a trick of mind or a coping technique. It is rather a spiritual and theological recognition of the partnership with Christ that I believe to be absolutely necessary if we are to minister freely and effectively. It is also a reminder that we ministers, too, live under grace. All God expects of us in a given day is that we do the best we can with the talents, time, and energy we are given. In the long term, a minister who cannot allow herself to receive God's grace at the end of the day will find that she cannot continue to serve. Ministry is simply too difficult. It will wear you down.

Because ministry is often a reactive occupation—that is, something happens and we respond—it's important as well to develop a strategy for coping through the day as you become aware of stressful events. Not every stress requires immediate action. Even if an emergency is in progress, we can often find a few moments to collect our thoughts, to "center down," as the Quakers would say, or to pray. Often in my own ministry, in response to a stressful event I would simply go to the sanctuary to pray. The quiet and the beauty of that place and the time for prayer usually gave me an opportunity to clear my head, to assess my feelings, and to organize my thoughts to respond appropriately to the challenge. It also helped sometimes to call a colleague or my wife and to talk through what had just happened. In hearing myself talk about the event, I often found clarity about what I needed to do next. The important thing is to have a coping strategy you're comfortable with and to use it.

Addressing Conflict

Conflict, one of the greatest sources of stress for clergy, is inevitable in ministry. It's inevitable because we ourselves are fallible, and we are dealing with fallible people. Sometimes we hurt people's feelings. Sometimes we disagree with the leaders or other members of the staff about vision or theology or expectations. Sometimes we are clumsy in the execution of our duties. Sometimes we simply dislike someone, or someone dislikes us. Nothing in Scripture suggests that liking everyone in the church is a requirement for Christian ministers. For these and a thousand other reasons, a competent minister needs to know how to deal with the stress of conflict.

Whole books have been written about how to manage conflict in the church and how to transform conflict into growth. Two that I have found particularly helpful are Joseph Phelps's *More Light, Less Heat*,[4] which deals with learning to engage in dialogue about controversial issues, and Carolyn Schrock-Shenk and Lawrence Ressler's *Making Peace with Conflict*, which provides a comprehensive set of prescriptions for dealing with various kinds of conflict.[5]

Both books recognize that differing levels of conflict exist within congregations. A competent minister will therefore develop a range of responses for managing situations. At the most basic level, conflicts arise because of simple misunderstandings or miscommunications. As we said in an earlier chapter, every minister needs to strive for clear communication. Along with that care in what we say and write initially, we must also develop the habit of going directly to the person concerned whenever there appears to have been a miscommunication.

Here's what I mean. Let's say that a funeral service with a printed order of worship is being prepared for a longtime member. You realize that you have conflicting notes from your conversations with the family about what image is to go on the cover—Psalm 23 or Jesus' words "I am the Resurrection and the Life." What do you do? Obviously, you call and ask again. Yet, although this answer seems self-evident, some ministers would agonize for hours, try to reconstruct the conversations in their mind, and generally make themselves miserable rather than pick up the phone.

At a more serious level, of course, you may find yourself in an ongoing personality conflict or difference of opinion with a member of the church. Most of us simply aren't put together to get along well with everybody. Indeed, if we do get along well with everybody, we probably won't be very effective in our work! Our natural tendency is to avoid or minimize contact with those we find difficult. I believe that is precisely the wrong thing to do.

Glen Stassen, professor of Christian ethics at Fuller Theological Seminary in Pasadena, California, has developed an interpretation of the Sermon on the Mount that addresses this point. Stassen argues that the unique element in Jesus' teachings in Matthew 5 is the "surprising, transforming initiative" the disciple is called to take. The law required one to carry a soldier's pack for a mile. Going the second mile would be a total surprise. It had the potential to remove one's victim status by offering voluntary rather than compulsory service and thereby to create an opportunity for dialogue.[6]

In a similar vein, I believe we should go out of our way to seek nonthreatening opportunities for fellowship with those in the church whom we dislike. Often people will sense an antipathy. But seeking out those we find difficult to deal with, spending time with them, and making a particular effort to be friendly can disarm a tense relationship. Avoiding those whom we dislike, on the other hand, which for many of us is the preferred strategy, merely increases the distance and creates potential for even more misunderstanding.

There is, of course, an even more serious level of conflict in the church—for example, when a group is unhappy with our leadership or is pursuing a policy decision we oppose. At this level, some form of intervention is often the best course to pursue. In one church I served, after about two years a representative of a small group came seeking to set up a meeting with me to "air our concerns." The members of this group were particularly attached to the previous pastor and were having trouble accepting me in that role.

Rather than meet with these people alone, an approach that felt unsafe to me, I brought in two additional people. One was the lay leader of the congregation. It seemed important to me to have him present to make sure that everything said would be "on the record." The second person I brought in was a pastoral counselor who knew and had been a consultant on the church's recent history. Her purpose was to serve as facilitator for the meeting and consultant to me about whatever subsequent action would need to be taken.

My purpose in structuring the meeting this way was twofold. I communicated to the group that I was indeed taking its concerns seriously. And I established a context of accountability in which all of us could be held responsible for the things we said. Conflict, I believe, is often best addressed in the presence of neutral and benevolent parties and those with particular expertise in personal interaction. Having those two extra people in our meeting reduced my stress level considerably and gave us a much more positive result than we would otherwise have achieved.

One part of competent ministry is knowing when you need help to address an issue. Generally speaking, it's always a good idea to consult those whom you trust in dealing with any issue. It's especially important to do so, however, whenever you feel unsure or threatened in any way.

Perhaps the key insight about conflict is that conflicts rarely go away if they are not addressed. They may lurk under the surface for a time, but they will inevitably come back to haunt us if we do not seek to achieve resolution or reconciliation. In the long term, the only way to reduce our stress level is to reduce the conflict.

Coping with Criticism

All ministers are subject to criticism. Sometimes it's fair. Sometimes it's not. But fair or not, criticism hurts. For many of us, the way we deal with criticism creates serious stress in our lives. Fifteen people on the way out of worship may tell us warmly, "Hey, Pastor, I really enjoyed that sermon today!" For most of us, the impact of their words will vanish before the people reach their cars. But, if the 16th says, "I really think you missed the point today," the words will haunt us for days or weeks, or even longer. Clearly there is a difference between being "sensitive" and being "touchy." The former enables us to respond to people's legitimate needs and wants. The latter makes us hypersensitive to every opinion that comes our way, no matter how eccentric or half-baked.

In learning to tell the difference between when to be sensitive and when not to be touchy, it's important to recognize that criticisms may or may not concern anything we can change. About 20 years ago a family told me they were attending less since I came as pastor because my eyes were too close together. I had a healthy enough self-image to recognize that surgery was out of the question as a pastoral response, but I still remember the jab. Obviously I'm a bit touchy about my appearance!

The key factor in coping with criticism then is making a clear decision about which criticisms we will listen to and which we will not. Some people we will never please. We can't please them because their displeasure *with* us is not *about* us. It is about them, their own mental, emotional, or spiritual health, or the circumstances of their lives. Early in my own ministry I had the great good fortune to have as a member of my congregation an extremely wise retired pastor. At one point I was describing to him my efforts to please a member of the congregation who simply refused to be pleased. He interrupted, somewhat dismissively, "Just put them on your crazy list!"

Taken aback, I asked for an explanation. He said, "There will always be people like that. I learned long ago that some people simply refuse to be helped. So, after I've listened and taken them seriously and made every reasonable effort, if nothing works, I put them on my crazy list, and then I don't have to worry about it anymore! I can love them in Christ and pray for them without having to take their criticisms to heart." Obviously it's not always that simple. Still, from time to time I remember the crazy list, and add a new name to the roster.

Anonymous critics are a particularly vicious subset of the critical. They set out to cause pain without bearing responsibility for their words. Sometimes

---

I had been in a congregation for a year or so. A task force of people got together to discuss changing the seating in our chapel to allow for more and flexible space. We planned carefully how we would introduce the idea. Some of the people who we thought might reflexively oppose the concept were invited to be on the task force. We agreed on a strategy.

One of the groups likely to be affected by the plan was the choir. A member of the task force, in error, hastily told the choir about the plan before we had a chance to use our strategy for communication. Some choir members reacted strongly to the proposed changes at their Thursday evening rehearsal. I didn't hear about it until Sunday morning, but when I did, I promptly went to their Sunday morning rehearsal and said that I wanted all of us to talk about this possible change. Then I explained it and

this kind of criticism comes in the form of a letter or a phone call. Sometimes church members will complain to a senior pastor about associates, or to associates about the senior pastor, and claim the privilege of confidentiality.

As a general principle, the best way to handle anonymous criticism in any form is not to give it the dignity of attention. If a letter comes, do not read it. If a church member wants to criticize another staff member to you confidentially, ask if the critic has spoken directly to the person. If not, refuse to listen. If he or she insists on confiding, make it clear that you will neither act upon nor carry anonymous tales. Criticism may well be legitimate, and we may need to hear it. Responsible criticism, however, always comes with a name and a face attached.

An alternative strategy for dealing with anonymous letters is to post them in a public place for church members to read. Often someone will be able to figure out who the author is. At a minimum, the anonymous critic loses the thrill of causing damage without at least the threat of having to accept responsibility for what he or she has done.

A second crucial factor in coping with criticism has to do with the attitude with which we hear criticism that comes to us by legitimate means. Even angry or mean-spirited criticism may contain a grain of truth we need to hear. It's important therefore to listen to criticism with a selective ear. We need to develop the ability to learn from criticism without letting it damage our self-esteem. Often even the most critical people do mean well. As the pastor of a congregation, I tried to maintain a connection with a

asked for their questions and input. As they heard the story, they opposed it less and became open to exploring the ideas. The person who had prematurely told them about the plan graciously apologized for the confusion, and I respected and thanked him for doing¯ that. The fire settled down immediately. I observed that the choir members were surprised that anyone would come directly and promptly to them with an issue. It spoke to them of my respect for their opinion and had a lasting effect beyond the chapel concerns. JM

How might we better love the unreasonable critic, even as we discipline ourselves not to stress out? Some years ago I developed a simple technique of silent prayer. As I listen to such a person or read what he or she has written, I force myself to pray without words and say to God: "Help me to remember that this is one of your beloved children." I find that the prayer calms me, restores perspective, and enables me to make better decisions. MAS

counselor or other professional with whom I could share the criticisms that came my way. They brought to the incidents an objectivity I could not achieve on my own. Not incidentally, they were also
usually very sympathetic. By filtering the criticism through another
person's perceptions I usually found it much easier to retain what I
needed to retain and to let go what I needed to let go.

Coping with the Stress of Failure

Virtually every minister experiences significant failure. I say "virtually" to allow for the remote possibility that somebody out there
somewhere may have somehow miraculously escaped what seems to
me a universal experience. For all practical purposes, though, coping with the stress of failure is a skill that all competent ministers
need to learn.

The first step when we fail in ministry is simply to acknowledge
the reality of the failure. Masking failure in excuses, blame-shifting,
or anger simply prolongs our self-imposed stress. Instead, this is a
moment to give ourselves the grace of acknowledging that Jesus
failed too. By any objective standard, his earthly ministry was a spec-
tacular failure. Yet out of that failure God brought redemption, and
God can redeem our failures too. Note what I did not say: I did not
say that God will turn our failures into successes. We're not talking
about rescue here. We're talking rather about endurance—about
going through the valley and coming out stronger on the other
side. When we allow our failures to turn us back toward Christ, we
create the potential for learning and growing from what we have
experienced.

The second step in coping with the stress of failure is to give
ourselves time and room to heal. Failure creates grief, and to some
extent when we fail, we go through all the stages of grief associated
with any other loss. Anger, denial, bargaining, depression, acceptance, and a readiness to move forward again all come into play. If
we attempt to short-circuit the process by moving ourselves too
quickly into some new project, we may set ourselves up to fail again.
Instead it's important to let the grieving process do its work. However painful the experience, sometimes it is only when we are coping
with failure that we see ourselves most clearly and get the best ideas
about areas of our behavior that we need to address.

Only as we feel ourselves moving out of the worst of our grief are we ready for this third step in coping with the stress of failure—learning from our failure so as not to repeat the same mistakes again. It takes a bit of distance and time to take this step. With my own biggest mistakes in ministry, I've found that a year or more may need to pass before I'm really ready to acknowledge my own role in creating the failure. That objectivity becomes a crucial ingredient in my self-analysis. Only when I'm able to look objectively at my own behavior can I begin to put into practice some positive strategies for preventing the same kind of failure the next time around.

The fourth step in coping with the stress of failure is doing it (whatever "it" is!) better the next time around. Sometimes, of course, we don't get a second chance. Surprisingly often in the ministry, however, similar situations do come around again. Success consists in learning from our previous failures so that we can both recognize when we are in danger of repeating failed strategies and alter our behavior to create the possibility for a better result.

Failure creates the opportunity for us to recapitulate in our own lives the gospel story. Themes of sin, grace, repentance, and the new life in Christ all come into play. Moreover, sometimes the stories of our failures and experiences of grace can become a meaningful part of our ministry to others. People fail a lot. They need to know that we as their clergy fail too, and that our faith in Christ sustains us when we do.

Sometimes, of course, the whole congregation fails. The annual stewardship drive may not fully fund the budget. The membership drive may yield few or no new participants in the church. The outreach program we thought would be so effective may not turn out as we'd hoped. In this kind of situation we must cope not only with the stress of our own failure but also with the compounding of that stress in the corporate experience of the congregation.

We must expect that the congregation will go through much the same process that we are experiencing ourselves. In one congregation I served, a capital-funding campaign fell short. We had hoped to raise the money for an extensive renovation of our building. When the pledging was done, however, we had only enough to proceed with architectural plans and to move forward with a few small projects. The members did their best to put a good face on the experience. But it was clear that everyone was bitterly disappointed. It took a couple of years for the project to regain the momentum we had lost. Whenever a church fails, all the stages of grief will apply. In some cases the congregation's anger may be directed at the pastor. In extreme cases the members' grief may cut us off from the opportunity of further ministry in that place. Congregations do occasionally sacrifice their minister upon the altar of a failed program.

More often, though, our job will be to serve as a nonanxious anchor for the congregation during the grief period. When we failed to raise enough money to proceed immediately with our whole renovation project, I worked to help the congregation celebrate what we had done and to help the leadership decide what we could actually do next. The key here is to maintain a balance between realism and hope. We must acknowledge the reality of our own grief, allow our people to grieve without feeling guilty for doing so, and then help them to analyze the failure, caring about them while they do so. Step by step we can help the congregation build a new history of achievement, based in part on what we have learned from our previous experience.

Coping with the Stress of Success

Success can be every bit as stressful as failure. One only has to listen to the testimonies of athletes or actors who find themselves suddenly thrust into the spotlight to realize that success has its challenges. For those of us in the ministry the stress of success comes in quite specific ways.

If we do well with our preaching, we create high expectations in our congregation. Knock one out of the park one Sunday, and they'll expect you to knock one out of the park the next Sunday too. Some ministers are in such demand as speakers that they have little time left for study and the other tasks of ministry.

A similar phenomenon takes hold when the church is growing. Suddenly everything seems to be about growth. Finding ways to accommodate new people, dealing with increased needs for staff, and coping with the inevitable organizational tensions associated with growth mean that both clergy and the congregation as a whole must constantly be adapting to new realities.

Perhaps most difficult in terms of the stress it creates is the reality that successful ministry tends to cultivate in the best of us an illusion of invincibility. From 30 years of observing the profession, I would say that one of the primary contributing factors when ministers cross sexual or ethical boundaries is the illusion that the rules that apply to everybody else somehow don't apply to us. Ministers with a string of successes may begin to think that success is somehow their due. It may become easy to confuse their wants with their rights. And when we think we have a right to something such as money or pleasure or power, it's only a small step from the thought to the deed.

One strategy more than any other offers promise for dealing competently with the stress of success. That strategy involves putting oneself under a consistent structure of accountability—something that may be especially difficult for a successful minister. Normal venues for ministerial fellowship, such as a denominational prayer group or a lectionary study group, may be marked by competition. A minister who is often in the public eye may be reluctant to share too much of himself or herself with peers.

In such a situation it becomes even more crucial that a minister locate and cultivate a safe venue for accountability. Most larger communities will have people who are trained as specialists in spiritual direction. Spiritual directors are bound by the same standards of confidentiality as professional counselors. Their role is twofold. First, they are to reflect to their clients an honest response to the client's self-revelation. They help us see ourselves through another Christian's eyes. Second, they are to point their clients toward healthy practical and spiritual disciplines. A competent spiritual director can help keep you grounded in the midst of a busy ministry.

When I was a senior pastor in a relatively new-to-me community, I sought out a counselor to hear my concerns and to help give me a sense of balance. She observed that single women, and especially single female senior pastors, were some of the loneliest people she had ever worked with. They lacked the support of family, were limited in how they could live out their personal social lives, and as senior pastors had to maintain at least some distance from their colleagues whom they supervised. For me it was invaluable to have someone offer correction to my faulty expectations or self-appraisal and to encourage me both as a person and a pastor. I suspect in this case it was useful that the counselor was of my gender as well. JM

Some ministers, whether they're particularly successful or not, prefer to see a professional counselor, Christian or otherwise. As a pastor I found it helpful to pay someone from time to time to listen to me. At least one congregation put money in the budget to pay for this kind of consultation for the entire ministerial staff. Many health insurance policies will also pay for a limited amount of counseling each year. In a setting of confidentiality, I could bring up any subject without worrying about how it would be received or where the information might end up. That relationship in itself constituted a structure of grace that allowed me to be honest about my own struggles.

Keeping in frequent and meaningful touch with a few trustworthy, wise friends may also meet the need described here. Genuine, cultivated friendships provide accountability. For example, one such friend serves a small mountain church in another state. He listens well, reflects carefully, and tells me precisely what he thinks. Over the years he has kept my feet on the ground in times of success or failure. Such friendships require an investment of initiative and time, but they may more than repay what is invested. MAS

When neither of these options is realistic, I believe that every minister should seek some kind of covenantal relationship of accountability. As a pastor, for example, you might seek out a hospital chaplain or other caring professional. Establishing a relationship of mutual accountability with a minister of another denomination often helps. For the successful minister a relationship of accountability, however one acquires it, helps keep you honest, spiritually grounded, and realistic about your own abilities and limitations.

Competent Stress Management

As the preceding pages indicate, the techniques for managing specific stressors in our lives are as varied as the stresses themselves. In some ways Joan, in our opening vignette, was quite lucky to experience such an obvious physical symptom of her stress. Her symptoms gave her a warning that she needed to make changes in her strategies for coping. Heart disease, by contrast, may give you no advance warning of a crisis at all. What is clear is that the same habits that serve us well apart from the stress of ministry also serve us well when ministry is the stressor. When we ministers mistakenly conclude that the basic rules of good health don't apply to us, we are ripe for stress-related damage. When we work to keep our bodies and our lifestyles healthy physically, mentally, emotionally, socially, and spiritually, we are able to handle the stresses of ministry appropriately as they arise.

For Further Reading

Wayne E. Oates and Roy M. Oswald have both written extensively on the subject of managing ministerial stress. You will find their works referred to throughout this chapter. In addition, the following books address significant issues of stress:

Bramson, Robert M. *Coping with Difficult People.* New York: Ballantine Books, 1981.

Rediger, G. Lloyd. *Clergy Killers. Guidance for Pastors and Congregations under Attack.* Louisville: Westminster John Knox, 1997.

SIX

Blessed Are the Peacemakers

Competent Interpersonal Skills

"Wow, that felt good! I hope I do that well with the elders tonight!" John Green congratulated himself and tossed a kind of half-prayer skyward at the same time. He was just getting back to his office after an hour's basketball with the senior high boys' group.

In his three years at Grace Church, the elders had been his biggest relationship challenge. At 35, John was a good 15 years younger than the youngest elder. His easygoing, lighthearted (well, OK, sometimes flippant) style seemed to rub several of them the wrong way. Last month, there'd been a particularly nasty exchange.

John wasn't really sure how it had started. Something in the way he referred to the question of whether the U.S. flag should be displayed in the sanctuary seemed to have touched a nerve in Edna Fever. Edna's husband, Joe, had died last year after a military career that spanned 30 years, and she was still grieving.

"You know," she said, holding her head rigidly high and clipping her words like the school administrator she had been, "it hardly seems appropriate to me that someone who's never served our country should presume to comment on proper reverence for Old Glory! With all due respect, John, what do you know about it?"

John's real mistake, he thought, was that he'd tried to answer. "Well, Edna, I was an international-relations major in college, and my seminary ethics training focused on the relation-ship of church and state. I do feel qualified in this area."

"Book learning!" She spit back, tears gathering in her eyes. "What do you know about the kind of suffering Joe went through in Vietnam? You'd probably have been marching against the war with those awful hippies!" With that, Edna swept from the room. After an embarrassed silence, the chair suggested that the discussion be tabled until next time, and the meeting stumbled on.

John had gone over the incident in his mind a thousand times since then. What could he have done better? What was really going on that night? Was this a generational problem? Should he have tried to deal with the issue in another venue? Should he have called Edna the next day? She'd barely spoken to him all month. She'd always been supportive until now. Was the relationship ruined forever? John just didn't know what to do.

Pastors deal with people. Write it inside the front cover of your Bible. This is the basic reality of the ministry as a vocation. Whatever we do in the church and the community inevitably requires us to relate to a variety of people. As I thought about how to approach this chapter on interpersonal competence, I considered writing about the diverse groups to which a minister must relate. A multiplicity of distinct groups are included in virtually every ministry—the old, the middle-aged, the young, church leaders, visitors, counselees, colleagues, antagonists, fans, and the public at large. A minister's skills must, of course, be honed and tailored for all these disparate groups.

At the same time, however, a core group of interpersonal skills seems to me applicable to every situation in which we clergy will find ourselves. These skills are both simple to name and difficult to practice. It's easy to say, for example, that a clergy member should be a good listener. But what does that mean? How is skillful listening different when you're dealing with a 16-year-old rather than a 70-year-old? With a female rather than with a male? When you're in a hospital room rather than on a basketball court? How is listening the same in each of these situations and a host of other situations as well? This chapter deals with what seem to me the key interpersonal skills for ministers, recognizing that only you can cultivate and adapt them as you pursue competence in your own situation.

Listening

Listening got me my wife. When we talked, years later, about the key qualities that attracted us to each other, she told me that what made her take a serious look at me was the way I seemed to be genuinely interested in her—her thoughts, her story, the things she considered important. When we went out, I asked her about herself. Apparently many of the men she'd dated before hadn't done that! The point of this story is not that I'm a terrific listener. Unfortunately, listening in ministry isn't at all like listening to the girl you want to marry. Indeed, it had better not be! And as my editor informs me, studies show that people tend to quit listening once they marry anyway. The point is that we connect with people by learning how to listen.

What constitutes competent listening for a minister? Many of us who become clergy do so in part because others perceive us as "good with people." We tend to assume that our skills include how to listen. Unfortunately many clergy tend in practice to be better talkers than listeners. Enjoying people does not necessarily make you good at listening. Fortunately, listening is a skill that can be learned and even enhanced. The dynamics of listening have been subjected to rigorous

Pioneer pastoral counselor Wayne Oates termed the pastor's attention to those in pain "the ministry of presence." In effect, you communicate grace in times of crisis by giving someone your undivided attention. JAH

analysis, particularly by psychologists and practitioners of pastoral care. Skills have been identified that can help us become better listeners. Works such as John Savage's *Listening and Caring Skills: A Guide for Groups and Leaders* contain a genuine treasury of helpful information for those who want to improve their listening skills.[1]

Let me offer a couple of key principles. *First, listening to others is* CARING *one of the primary ways pastors communicate caring*. People need to know that they are important to us. We communicate that they are important by being interested in their stories. Savage reports that 7 percent of a communication consists in what is said, 38 percent in the speaker's tone of voice, and 55 percent in posture and body language. [2] If that is true, consider how much we ministers communicate in the way we receive our people's stories.

Do you listen "on the way" to a more important meeting? Do you turn your body away as someone begins a boring story? Do you keep from making eye contact to discourage further confidences from some people? Do you interrupt another's story with one of your own about a similar experience? Do you primarily wait for opportunities to teach, correct, solve a problem, or turn the attention to yourself? A competent minister commits herself to the principle that people are worth hearing and that their stories are important. That does not mean we don't set boundaries to how and when we will listen. Some people do go on ad nauseam, and some people are truly boring. They represent special cases, and at certain times, it would be irresponsible for us to turn our attention to an individual. The five-minute interval before the beginning of worship is not the moment to tell me every detail of your recovery from gall-bladder surgery. If I am your pastor, however, I will want to hear how you are doing, and I will carve out sufficient time to hear you. A competent pastor will work to cultivate the art of listening as a primary tool in pastoral care.

The second key principle, then, with regard to listening is that listening skills and techniques can be learned. Let's examine a couple of these skills by way of example.

The first skill Savage discusses is "paraphrasing." By that he means "the act of saying back to the speaker in your own words what you heard the person say."[3]

It's a simple technique, but it comes in handy in any number of pastoral contexts. I learned quickly in counseling parishioners that what I heard them say might not be at all what they meant to say. Often the best way to check my perception was to summarize briefly what I'd heard. Usually they would then either say, "That's right!" and go on to the next part of their story, or say, "No, that's not what I meant!" and try again to help me understand.

Paraphrase is also useful in working on projects or in committees. I learned through the years that one of the best things for me to do as a church committee meeting drew to a close was to summarize for the group my understanding of what we had decided. Of course, a competent committee chair would do this for me! But if

SAYING BACK what was said

no one else did so, I took the initiative to allow all present the opportunity to check their perceptions of what had happened.

Ministers find paraphrase useful also when we're acting as a sounding board for church people. Often when people came to me upset or frustrated, I would sit down with them, listen to their story, and then say something like, "So, you're frustrated with our choir director, and you don't think you can sing for him even one more Sunday!" Hearing those words would often provide a kind of reality check for the complainer. He or she might answer, "You're exactly right. I've had it!" Or: "No, I was just letting off steam. I really do love to sing, and he's not that bad." Often when people come to us, they will solve their own problem. They simply want us to listen and to care about them in the listening. By doing so we create a healing space within which their own inner wisdom can be heard. Learning to practice paraphrase is one way to do that.

A second critical listening skill involves learning to read and respond to the body language and tone of voice of those who come to us for counseling and of those whom we encounter in our daily rounds. We all know that body language communicates. We all know that tone of voice can completely alter the meaning of a sentence. To a certain extent we grow up reading other people's body language and responding to their tone of voice, and most of us assume that we can do that adequately. But if Savage is right that these two factors together provide 93 percent of the content of any communication, our ability to read that communication accurately becomes a crucial pastoral skill.

Savage calls this skill a "perception check."[4] Let's say, for example, that John and Marsha come to you for premarital counseling. When they enter your study, John sits on the furthest point of the couch from you, crosses his arms, and looks straight ahead. Marsha sits next to him, but turns her body toward you, smiles, and catches your eye. If this posture continues past the first couple of minutes, it might be appropriate to say to John something like "John, I wonder how you feel about this premarital counseling process?" This kind of gentle question gives a counselee the opportunity to verbalize what he might be feeling and gives you a chance to check out your perception about his body language. Whether they intend to or not, people are constantly offering us clues to their emotional and spiritual states, simply by the way they walk, stand, sit, use their hands, hold their head, speak, and so on. The better we get at reading that unspoken language, the better listeners we will become. Note, though, that it's dangerous to assume that you know how someone is feeling merely on the basis of body language. If at all possible, it's far better to do a perception check.

Supporting

A second major interpersonal skill for clergy is offering caring support for others. Wayne Oates, in his classic text *The Christian Pastor,* talks about this function in several ways, among them "friendship" and "comfort."[5]

Cojourner

In general, a pastor supports the flock simply as a Christian brother or sister, a fellow traveler along the Christian road. Oates points out that this function is reflected in the custom in many rural Protestant congregations of calling the pastor "Brother." People expect their minister to be living the Christian life alongside them, and they look to their minister to take a personal interest in them and in the way their Christian pilgrimage is progressing.

This "friendship along the Christian way" sounds easy, but it is not necessarily so. Your personality plays a crucial role here. As an "introverting thinker" (see chapter 2) from a sometimes less-than-supportive family, I found that expressing consistent, supportive interest in other people's struggles does not come naturally for me. Instead, displaying supportive interest is a skill I have found it necessary to cultivate. When someone tells me about a problem, I have to think to say, "I will pray for you." I will then write that person's name on my calendar to remind myself to pray, and make a note on the calendar for a week or so later to remind myself to check on him. In my tradition the church prays for those in need on Sunday mornings and Wednesday evenings. I ask if it's OK to mention the person's name to the congregation, and then, depending on the situation, I may also suggest that a deacon or elder join me as part of a caring team to keep up with her while the need continues. This kind of expressed caring is a significant factor in helping people feel comforted and supported.

It's important to learn to express caring in everyday interactions with the church. Perhaps you're calling church member Rhett Tyree about some business for the church property committee. For someone with my personality, the natural course of my half of the conversation might go something like this: "Hi, Rhett! How are you? Good! I wanted to talk about getting the roof fixed over the chapel entry. Can you take care of that before Sunday? You can? Good! Thanks a lot! See you then! Bye!" Is there a problem with that kind of exchange? Not necessarily, but there may be. It depends on your history and relationship with Rhett. Have you shown personal interest in him in the past? Is he dealing with some difficult personal or health issue? Does he need a particular kind of encouragement?

Pastoral conversation needs to display a consistent, warm personal interest in the welfare and growth of those with whom we deal. The conversation with Rhett might have needed to go very differently. Suppose Rhett's answer to my first question was, "Oh, Pastor, it's a rough week. My arthritis is acting up and I can barely climb the stairs." In that event, my agenda would need to change radically. The job I want Rhett to do takes a back seat, and I go into caring mode. "Oh, I'm sorry to hear that! Have you been to the doctor? . . ." It's possible that we might still get around to talking about the roof of the chapel entrance, but caring becomes my primary task for the conversation. One of the most damning things a parishioner can say about their pastor is "She doesn't really care about me. She just wants to be sure I show up to teach that class." And, indeed, once people begin to say such things about us, it's extremely difficult to change that perception. To put it simply, a competent minister takes a consistent, friendly interest in the life and faith of those in the parish.

A second level of support comes into play whenever church folk have a crisis. By that I mean a death or a life-changing or life-threatening event. At this level, the minister's task is to be present, to listen, and to offer the comforts of the faith. In case of a death, for example, a pastor will go immediately to the hospital or the home to be with the family of the one who has died. By that simple ministry of presence, the pastor symbolizes the concern of the whole congregation. Over the days between the death and the funeral, the pastor contacts the family frequently, listening as family members talk about the one who has died and come to grips with the reality of the death. When appropriate, the pastor offers words of comfort and points to the hope of the Christian faith.

It's also important in a bereavement or crisis situation to pay attention to more mundane needs. A crisis may cause people to lose sleep or aggravate health problems. The pastor may be the only person in a position to ask, "Are you eating? Are you sleeping OK? Do you need to check with your doctor?" There may be errands to be run or details to be taken care of. Offering to do those specifics, or to find someone in the church to do them, can be a significant help.

When we enter a hospital room or a home, we can do a visual assessment of the room and form meaning from what we see. Is the room clean or cluttered? Are there flowers or cards around the sickbed? What is the attitude of those present? By observing details we can inform our own ministry. JAH

One of the tricks here is to recognize that members may need support long after we think they should. Part of John Green's problem in this chapter's opening vignette was that he failed to recognize the danger signs when Edna began to react to the proposal about the flag in the sanctuary. A year after a spouse dies is often only the beginning of a mourning period after a long marriage. Edna's tone and posture should have helped John realize that this was an issue on which she did not need reasoned dialogue. She needed rather to know that her pastor and her church would continue to show proper respect for her husband and his career. Chances are, John would have gotten much further with Edna had he spent at least a bit of time talking about the church's debt to veterans and how that debt would be acknowledged on a regular basis.

Much of a pastor's life is spent learning to recognize when and how to offer appropriate comfort to those in the congregation. Specific and detailed help in developing such skills lies beyond the scope of this book. However, I highly recommend the works of Wayne E. Oates as one place to find such assistance. One of the founders of the pastoral care movement in American religion, Oates spent a long and distinguished career at the Southern Baptist Theological Seminary in Louisville and the University of Louisville. He wrote copiously on topics of practical use to parish ministers. For example, his work *Grief, Transition, and Loss: A Pastor's Practical Guide* (Minneapolis: Fortress, 1997) speaks directly to problems such as the one John encountered with Edna.

Collaborating

Ministers work with people. <u>Competent ministers balance personal</u> *It doesn't have to look like how I would do it*
<u>responsibility for their own performance with including others in</u>
<u>working together toward the church's common goals.</u>

For a lot of us, this balance doesn't come easily. Collaboration, the skill of working well with others, is taught in contemporary American schools from kindergarten onward. Often, however, the personality types of people attracted to the ministry and the academic self-discipline required to prepare for a ministerial vocation work against our developing a collaborative mind-set for ministry. I, for example, as a strong introvert with a love of getting things done, often find it much easier to work alone. By myself I can put together an annual stewardship emphasis in a few hours. Working with a committee, that process can take months. But the committee work is essential for the church's ownership of the emphasis, whether I can do it more efficiently alone or not.

<u>Ministers cannot and should not approach the work of the church as lone rangers.</u> As long as you do everything, the congregation is not learning to take responsibility for the members' own Christian service. In the little pastors' manual *The Penguin Principles*, David Belasic and Paul Schmidt take a fascinating perspective on this issue. One of the basic principles of pastoral leadership, they say, is the principle of "creative ignorance"[6]—by which they mean it's often better for the pastor not to be competent at everything that needs doing around the church. <u>When pastors overfunction by doing everything themselves, they actually keep laypeople from growing in their Christian service</u>. It's far better, for example, to involve members with mechanical skills in keeping the boiler working or servicing the church van than it is for the pastor to do those things alone. In addition, focusing on that kind of detail can keep a minister from giving proper attention to the spiritual work of the ministry. Biblically, of course, this is how the office of deacon began (Acts 6:1-6). The apostles chose the first seven deacons to do the work of waiting tables to save their own time for preaching and teaching.

So how does a minister become competent at collaboration? Develop the mind-set of doing alone only those things that are your proper responsibility. Obviously sermon preparation is your job. (Even there, though, you can ask church members to pray for you on sermon-preparation day. And some pastors meet with groups of people who study the texts and talk with them about their own understanding and experience.) Counseling, visitation, and other properly "pastoral" functions can often be done in concert with others. Laypeople can be trained to undertake pastoral care with you. Occasions may arise when someone wishes to counsel with the pastor alone. But laypeople can also be extremely effective in caring for community folk along with you. Look for ways to collaborate as much as possible in all the work of the church. Whether your church functions with standing committees or the newer "ministry team" concept or some other configuration, most congregations are formally organized in such a way that the members are responsible for the work of the church. Your job is to work with them in making that formal responsibility a reality. When it's someone else's job, don't do it! Just as you're about to shift into problem-solving mode, stop yourself. Ask yourself, "For the good of the church, should I be the one to do this?" If your honest answer is that this would be better done in collaboration, take the extra time to think about how to make that collaboration happen. Call the appropriate people. Work with them. Help them. But do not focus on "getting it done." Focus instead on the process of working with others.

For many of us, this empowering of the congregation is ultimately a control issue. To empower others, we need to give up control ourselves. Ministers like to be in charge. Often we like to set the church's agenda and the direction of its ministry. Wanting to be in charge is an occupational hazard. But we have to remember that the church is never ultimately ours to control. Lifelong Presbyterian pastor John Galloway, Jr., deals with this concept with humor in his *Ministry Loves Company: A Survival Guide for Pastors.* A church, he says, is like a family reunion.[7] We as ministers are by definition not part of the family. We may well have a better potato salad to offer than the one Aunt Bessie has been making people sick with for years.

> Be responsible *for* yourself and responsible *to* others. Ministers often take on a responsibility that properly belongs to someone else. Being responsible *to* others confronts them with their own responsibility *for* themselves. JAH

But it's their family reunion. If they want to keep serving Aunt Bessie's salad, who are we to interfere?

On the other hand, we do play an important role in church guidance. A somewhat differently nuanced perspective from Galloway's is offered by a group of Texas ministers, Jim Herrington, Mike Bonem, and James Furr, in *Leading Congregational Change*.[8] In their work with revitalizing dead or dying congregations, they argue that creating dissatisfaction with the status quo is a prime pastoral responsibility. If Aunt Bessie's potato salad really has been making people sick, somebody, sometime needs to say so. And that task often falls to the pastor. Both perspectives, however, seem to agree that the key is the development of and agreement upon a congregational vision for ministry. The minister's job is to work with the congregation to discover what the members together believe God is calling them as a congregation to do. The minister then becomes a kind of coach, keeping the team working together and focused together toward the commonly held goal.

Collaboration isn't easy, but competent ministers develop the skill.

Confronting

Although collaboration is a difficult interpersonal skill to learn for ministry, learning to confront people is, for many of us, even more difficult. By confrontation I mean dealing directly with members of the congregation about disagreements or unpleasant truths. We ministers are by nature people pleasers. We want to be kind. We want to get along. We want people to like us. We don't want to quarrel. Some of us harbor deep in our souls an unspoken suspicion that Jesus might have lived longer if he'd made more of an effort to get along. For years my own deep aversion to conflict, combined with some unhealthy family-of-origin patterns, made me a kind of scorched-earth confronter. Like an army that destroys the opponent utterly, I would, when I confronted, set out to defeat the other person at all costs. I would avoid a confrontation as long as possible, stifling my hostilities until the pressure became too much to bear and the anger spilled out like molten lava, devastating everyone in its path. This technique was not good for pastoral ministry. Nor was it productive in any other relationship.

Fortunately for me, I married a woman from a much healthier family background. No subject was taboo. Her family would argue about anything and everything in the car or around the family din-

---

Confrontation is the business of unpacking personal information and/or projections with regard to someone else. You learn the difference between your assumptions about someone else and the reality. JAH

---

ner table without animosity or lasting repercussions. She demanded that kind of openness from me, and over the years I've learned to be much better at it. But I'm by no means "there" yet. Respectful, direct confrontation, I believe, is one of those skills we work on all our lives. Unfortunately, pastors need to become at least minimally competent in this area fairly quickly. Otherwise, we set ourselves up for frustrating ministry and potentially disastrous interaction with others. If you know you have a problem with this kind of interaction, it's a good idea to look for help in cultivating your confrontation skills immediately.

Fortunately, much is being written about matters related to confrontation. I have previously cited Joseph Phelps's book *More Light, Less Heat*, which deals particularly with church conflict related to social issues. From a pastoral care perspective, longtime seminary professor Andrew Lester has written a fascinating book, *The Angry Christian*.[9] In it Lester seeks to provide a new conceptual model for dealing with parishioners' anger. Pastoral care books such as Oates's *The Christian Pastor* commonly provide techniques for pastoral counseling, helping people come to grips with their own problems in a nonthreatening and therapeutic fashion. It's essential to keep reading in this field.

Here are a few simple techniques I've learned about when and how to use confrontation in our day to day work of ministry.

First, handle minor matters along the way. Much of our difficulty in interpersonal relations arises when we let a trifling misperception or miscommunication go unacknowledged rather than clarifying it immediately. For many of us, our regional culture works against us here. People in both the South and the Midwest in the United States place a high value on "being nice" or "getting along." For those of us raised in those cultures, our first impulse is often to swallow a disagreement rather than deal with it. The problem in ministry, of course, is that minor matters have a way of becoming major.

Consider, for example, the day-to-day dynamics of a pastor working with a church secretary. Pastors commonly determine the content of the Sunday bulletin. Secretaries commonly prepare the bulletin for distribution. It is important that bulletins be accurate. An incorrect hymn number or an error in a litany may disrupt the flow of worship. If a pastor discovers a significant error after the bulletin is already printed, should she let it go, mention it only to the secretary, make a public correction in the worship service, or ask that the bulletin be reprinted? The correct answer varies according to the specific circumstance. Many church secretaries are also church members—and that adds an extra layer of complication to the dynamic. What is clear, though, is that in most situations, a pastor who allows repeated inaccuracies to appear in the worship bulletin will face criticism from the congregation. In as nonthreatening a manner as possible, the pastor needs to communicate the importance of accuracy, hold the secretary accountable for accuracy, and provide whatever backup or training may be needed to make sure that consistent accuracy can be achieved. Obviously something like bulletin accuracy is a minor matter (except to the English teachers and perfectionists in the church!), but it can absorb enormous amounts of energy if not dealt with appropriately.

Second, don't assume that an issue will go away if you do nothing. In our opening vignette, John's major mistake in his interaction with Edna was failing to go back to her to express his pastoral concern. It's sometimes difficult to time this kind of interaction, but certainly a call or visit the next day would have been appropriate, given Edna's distress the night before. Often church members will feel embarrassed and awkward after a confrontation like the one in the deacons' meeting. John and Edna may both wish they could avoid speaking about the matter again. That makes it even more important for John to take the initiative. Members may be afraid that we're angry with them. They may begin telling the story to others in an attempt to drum up support for their position. A swift, direct, and personal expression of concern on our part is the best way to handle such a situation.

Notice that I did not suggest a continuation of the discussion. John may well have been correct in his view of the issue, but that is not what is at stake here. What is at stake is his pastoral relationship with Edna. He needs to express concern for her, and to apologize for upsetting her. I have often found that a carefully worded apology, even when I don't think I've done anything wrong, can open the door to a fruitful and healing conversation.

③ Third, seek counsel when confronting major issues. From time to time in almost every pastorate, it will become necessary for you to confront a member over matters of church policy or, in many communions, church discipline. I have written previously about the value of maintaining an ongoing relationship with a professional psychologist, pastoral counselor, or judicatory representative outside your congregation who can advise you when a major issue arises. Let me repeat that advice here. Often an issue that appears major to us may not appear so to a more objective observer. We may gain a vital perspective simply by telling someone else about our frustration. By the same token, when that outside advisor agrees that we need to move forward with confrontation, or take some other action or actions, we are able to do so with greater confidence.

I had the opportunity of taking a "Healthy Congregations" workshop. The author Peter Steinke has prepared materials that help congregation members observe themselves and their issues in a nonanxious way, with some level of detachment. The workshops can be immensely helpful in the midst of a congregational conflict or as a preventive measure. JM

④ Fourth, consider what is at stake. In one pastorate I became aware of an extramarital affair among powerful members of the congregation. My personal moral convictions told me that such a situation must be confronted. My own relative newness in the congregation—and the power the offenders and their extended families held in the congregation and community— told me that such a confrontation would be filled with peril both for me personally and for the congregation. If the congregation became embroiled in a

When we deal with what is at "stake" in a crisis, we're talking about something valuable to us. In any given situation, ask, "Who are the stakeholders? What's at stake for you as pastor? What's at stake for those having the affair? What's at stake for the church as a whole? What's at stake for the church's children?" JAH

power struggle, I could even be fired—and that would cost our family both our livelihood and our place to live. After consulting several people we trusted, my wife and I finally decided that I must go ahead, because the very integrity and witness of the church of Jesus in that place were at stake. It was the most painful and frightening thing I have ever done in ministry. But what was at stake was too important not to do it.

Fifth, follow biblical guidelines, but watch your back. More often than not in church life, the structure for confrontation given by Jesus in Matthew 18 is acknowledged, but ignored in practice. The losing party in a power struggle complains bitterly that the winner failed to follow the instruction to go to the offender privately and to give that person a chance to make it right.

I firmly believe that most church members mean well, even when they are in the wrong. I also firmly believe that most people will respond well when their minister approaches them directly and kindly. We can say many difficult things so long as people know that we care deeply about them and have their best interests at heart. I also believe, however, that Jesus suggests differing techniques in Matthew 18 precisely because he knew how messy interpersonal dynamics can get.

Most often, you will confront someone privately. Relatively simple issues with one other person are best dealt with between the two of you. However, a minister will often find that confrontational conversations take place best with a third party present as a witness. At a low level of difficulty, such conversations may take place over lunch at a local restaurant. In the course of a wide-ranging discussion, you and the chair of the deacons can talk with finance committee member Bill Ding concerning his reservations about the proposed addition to the church. More difficult conversations may require increased levels of privacy as well as guidance from others. You may on occasion want to bring in an outside consultant to facilitate the exchange.

We should never be afraid, however, to address a difficult issue simply because it is difficult. If you reach the point in your relationship with a congregation at which a difficult issue cannot be addressed under your leadership, then you have reached the point when it is time for you to go.

Finally, pray. We Christian ministers must never forget that interpersonal relationships in the church never involve simply ourselves and the member of the church with whom we are dealing at the moment. The Holy Spirit wants very much to be part of the action. Again and again in ministry I have seen seemingly insurmountable difficulties melt away when those of us involved actively sought the Spirit's guidance in our situation.

Wayne Oates describes paying attention to the role of the Holy Spirit in pastoral conversations as moving the situation from a dialogue to a trialogue. JAH

Problem Solving

When we're not specifically involved in conflict, we're often involved in problem solving. On the one hand, church life is about problem solving: How do we get more parking? Can we afford to hire a youth minister? What do we do for the shut-ins this Easter? How much snow does there have to be before we cancel services? These problems and a thousand others are the stuff of which day-to-day church life is made. Many of us ministers thrive on this kind of detail. As task-oriented problem solvers ourselves, we feel fulfilled and productive whenever we check another issue off our list.

On the other hand, problem solving in the church is seldom that simple. John Green thought he knew exactly what should be done about the U.S. flag in the church sanctuary. He proposed a straightforward, theologically grounded solution. What he failed to take into account was the powerful mixture of cultural patriotism and personal loyalties that had led to placing and keeping that flag in the sanctuary for so many years. In "solving" one "problem," he created a host of others.

Thus is it always. As I entered my last pastorate, the church's chapel, which was used primarily for weddings and funerals, hadn't been redecorated in 40 years. It had fixed pews with dust-laden, deteriorating cushions, peeling green paint, poor lighting, a dilapidated organ, an old piano, an antiquated sound system and a carpet that had long since lost its original color. It was clear to me, without much thought, that we should simply strip that place and start over.

But notice I said "without much thought." The more deeply we got into the issue, the clearer it became that powerful constituencies within the church were working against significant change. Consider the pews. From my perspective, what we really needed was a more versatile room, one with attractive movable chairs that could be used either for worship or for various kinds of group meetings. But some members of the committee had been married in that room. Removing the pews would take away that visual reminder of a significant event in their lives. Not only that: the woman whose Sunday school class had made those pew cushions 40 years ago was now an octogenarian but still active in the church. And she came from a powerful, vocal family. Were we going to be so insensitive as to negate her contribution? In addition, there was within the church a powerful "traditional worship" lobby. This group tended to distrust movable chairs on principle as the first step on the slippery slope to contemporary perdition. After more than a decade of conversation, with the money in the bank to undertake the renovation, the pews are still there.

So how do you solve a problem in a way that pays adequate attention to interpersonal dynamics? There is a way. It's slow and difficult and often tricky, but it can be done. The first thing to remember is that in the church, process is almost always at least as important as product. By "process," I mean the way you go about making a decision. With regard to something like redecorating the chapel, for example, the best way to proceed is to involve everyone with a stake in the outcome at some level in the decision-making process. Such a process need not be terribly cumbersome. You could announce a congregational meeting chaired by the property committee. The purpose of the meeting might be "to get input from everyone interested in the redecoration of the chapel." You could solicit written comments from those uncomfortable speaking out in a meeting. The pastor could then make personal visits to individuals with a high stake in the process. The woman whose Sunday school class made the pew cushions would be

John Green's situation reminds us of the divide between a church's theology and its sociology. Successful ministers are not only good theologians but skilled sociologists! For example, my own tradition espouses separation of church and state. At the same time, many of the hymns the members love to sing on Memorial Day and Fourth of July weekends blur the line. What ought I to do? In this case, I've chosen to address the theological issue via sermons and in teaching settings while joining the congregation in singing their beloved hymns. In this way, I get a hearing because my congregation believes I accept them, even if I sometimes challenge their assumptions. MAS

one obvious person to visit in this situation. The key is that every important constituency gets an opportunity to be heard.

A second key point to remember is that ~~progress in the church~~ is ~~often incremental~~. In the chapel, for example, we were able to upgrade the organ, get a new piano, improve the lighting, and install a new sound system, even though we couldn't resolve the decorating issues. These improvements made for a more functional and inviting room, even though we did not do everything I would have liked. We did the elements of the project on which the most people were able to agree.

The third truth about problem solving, of course, is that you can never please everyone. There will be times when the church simply must move forward, even without full agreement on what needs to be done. In many church polities, the senior minister will have to decide when to push ahead—and leadership always comes at a cost. As a matter of discernment, the pastor will often have to decide when to push and when to let the process work without interference. The yardstick I used in making such a decision was always the overall welfare and witness of the congregation. If I believed an initiative would make us significantly stronger as a congregation, I was willing to spend an appropriate amount of my "political capital" to move the process forward.

Recruiting

I've chosen the relatively neutral term "recruiting" to characterize the twofold process of bringing new people into the fellowship of your church and encouraging those already in the church to participate fully in its life of fellowship and service. "Evangelism," "outreach," and "assimilation" are also frequently used to describe aspects of this process. Clearly pastors cannot and should not pursue these ventures alone. They are to be the work of the whole church, and a significant portion of what a pastor does in both aspects of recruiting should be "equipping the saints" for the work of ministry.

My purpose here is not to prescribe an approach that competent ministers should always use. Obviously Christian churches exist for the purpose of bringing people into relationship with Jesus Christ. It's equally obvious that there's no universal program that works everywhere for bringing people into the church. And there are dozens, if not hundreds, of such programs suggested by churches, denominations, and parachurch groups around the country. It's fair to say that the American church is focused on this issue perhaps more than any other practical aspect of congregational life. At the same time, surveys show that at any one time the vast majority of American congregations have numerically either reached a plateau or gone into decline.

Instead, I want to discuss the way the minister's personality and approach affect whatever methods of recruiting the churches you serve may adopt. As I noted above, it is necessary that the clergyperson like people. You don't have to like everybody. Nobody does. But a competent pastor does need to enjoy the process of getting to know people and discovering their needs, gifts, and abilities. You'll also be better at both phases of recruitment if you enjoy "Christian friendship," discussed above—the process of coming alongside a fellow pilgrim as companion, encourager, and friend. If you are either so extroverted that you feel compelled to tell other people what to do or so introverted that you have no interest in discovering others' lives and issues, you will not do well at recruiting new participants for the church or encouraging current members to welcome them and reach out to others.

The best way I've found to talk about how we recruit new believers is called "friendship evangelism." Essentially, a pastor or any other Christian takes an interest in someone he or she meets in the ordinary course of life. You seek to get to know them. You become their friend. In the process, you discover their likes and dislikes, strengths and weaknesses, spiritual and psychological needs. As appropriate, over time, you look for ways to engage them in conversation about what it means to be a follower of Jesus. Whether they make such a commitment or not, you continue to be their friend. As pastors we can practice friendship evangelism ourselves, as well as teaching the technique to the congregation. It's important also to note that in many traditions recruiting new believers and recruiting new members for the church are not the same thing. Sometimes new believers come from within the church fellowship itself. Sometimes people become believers without necessarily ever becoming "members" of the church.

Often, of course, this kind of relationship building may take place within the context of pastoral visitation of people who have visited your church. Relationship building can also happen in all kinds of other venues, from Wal-Mart to the swimming pool. Many churches have programs for visiting newcomers to the community. Others seek to build relationships with people whose children attend the church's programs or who use the church's facilities for recreation. Ministers frequently find themselves being asked to perform weddings for people who have no previous relationship with the church, or to counsel someone in crisis. Many ministers take part in community activities such as service clubs or school events. In fact, the more you as pastor build relationships in the broader community, the more the congregation will feel empowered to follow your example.

The key principles in recruiting people are that you genuinely enjoy getting to know them, that you look for ways to be of service to them as a Christian, that you be willing to speak specifically about the faith when appropriate, and that you continue to care about them even if they never join your church. In my formal role of visiting "prospects" for the churches I served, I would sometimes find as I got to know someone that the person was more conservative or more liberal, or would prefer a style of worship different from what our church could offer. In those cases, I often felt free to suggest to people that they try a neighboring congregation that might better meet their needs. It's more important to help someone find the place in the kingdom that's personally appropriate than it is to add one more number to the membership roll of your church.

It's especially important, I believe, that we not make it easier than it ought to be for people to become part of the church of Jesus. "Discipleship" implies discipline. That means those of us who do the recruiting for the church need to be careful to communicate to people what is expected of them if they choose to follow Christ. One new member who genuinely understands and accepts what is entailed in becoming a disciple is of more value to the kingdom of God in general and your congregation in particular than 10 who become members without such an understanding. Members who are not disciples tend to fall by the wayside when they encounter life's ups and downs.

The process of ministerial caring, then, does not entail becoming "all things to all people" in the sense of saying or doing whatever you need to say or do to recruit someone for the church. It does mean searching for appropriate means of caring for those whom you encounter while at the same time representing to them an authentic picture of the nature of Christian faith and life.

Of course, for the pastor of a congregation, much of day-to-day life will be caught up in working to encourage the people who are already part of the congregation in the ongoing fellowship and service of the church. This is the second essential phase in recruiting. Like the first, it cannot be done by the minister alone. Rather you will want to cultivate a community of encouragement and discernment. Members need to be about the process of mindfully inviting and including participation by newcomers.

Your role as minister is to facilitate the process of encouraging people to use their gifts. As a senior minister, I frequently found myself needing to ask someone to serve on a key committee or to undertake the shepherding role of a deacon (elder) or to help with a special project. I also dealt with many groups within the congregation that were also recruiting for various ministries. Congregations generally do this in one of two ways. Either they make a general announcement: "We need a volunteer to keep the nursery during Wednesday prayer meeting." Or they go to the person they think best and say, "Edith, you're so good with children. Would you consider keeping the nursery on Wednesday evenings?" General announcements often do little good. Getting to know people, discovering their gifts and abilities, and encouraging them to use those gifts tend to get a much better response.

Many congregations have found it useful in recent years to reduce and simplify their committee structures, going to a "team" approach to ministry. Teams may seek to staff specific projects for a limited time, or in the case of core functions of the church, they may be ongoing ministries. The use of short-term teams recognizes that busy people are much more likely to commit to a six-week team project preparing to welcome a refugee family than to a three-year term on a standing committee for missions. A general announcement, "We have openings on our technology team," may elicit a response from those interested in the electronic aspects of contemporary worship.

> Another term for such short-term groups is "task force." By definition they have a short, task-limited assignment. JM

Some congregations that have done the best job of welcoming newcomers have a policy of asking people to help with simple tasks as soon as they walk in the door. This kind of recruiting is not usually done by the pastor but rather by the team members themselves or by members who are especially gifted in this kind of inclusion.

Some congregations ask new members to serve as greeters before and after services. It allows them to meet people and to participate in a less demanding ministry. JM

Still there will be many times when the pastor needs to ask someone to serve. It may be that the specific task requires a particular level of expertise or needs to be done by someone who has the respect of the congregation, or that an individual who has not yet found a niche in the fellowship needs to be included. In these cases, the pastor will often be the one who should ask.

In doing this kind of direct recruiting, normally ask privately and face to face. Never do it over the telephone, by message or e-mail, or by letter, unless the person's schedule is such that you can't find a time to meet with her. If you can't find a time, that may suggest the person is too busy to do the job! In asking directly, you are able to convey to the person both the importance of the task and the reason you believe he should consider it. You offer people the simple respect of your time and energy in taking the trouble to see them. And, generally speaking, they will find it more difficult to dismiss your request out of hand. It's important, however, that we never attempt to pressure or manipulate anyone into taking on a responsibility. Follow your face-to-face meeting with a letter confirming the invitation and giving a job description and any other pertinent information about the task. Don't ask for a commitment at the meeting itself. Give the person time to think it over.

At times, congregations hope to involve people in the ministries of the congregation by having a person manage a "volunteer ministry" position. This approach has possibilities, but often fails because those people who desire such assistance don't go to the director or follow through with good support and training. It's possible that it is more effective to have one-on-one contacts than an organized system. JM

As you make these kinds of requests, of course, be certain to listen carefully to what someone says to you in response. Often in these conversations, we learn things about people that we did not know. The reason someone gives for turning you down may tell you something crucial about her family or her own spiritual condition. You may find that someone is saying "Yes!" when the things he's telling you or his body language or tone of voice suggest strongly that his answer should be "No!" Getting the tasks of the church done is never as important as caring authentically for the people.

Assessing Your Interpersonal Skills

Many of us spend all our lives assessing and working on our interpersonal skills. Many of us find that our spouses and children insist on it! Fortunately, trial and error is not the only way to move forward in this area.

A growing body of literature on the subject dates back to Dale Carnegie's classic *How to Win Friends and Influence People*. For a minister, working on interpersonal skills may begin with a step as simple as a trip to the self-help section of the bookstore. Two perennials in interpersonal skills that are still selling are Robert Bolton's *People Skills: How to Assert Yourself, Listen to Others and Resolve Conflict* (New York: Touchstone, 1986); and Don Gabor's *How to Start a Conversation and Make Friends*, revised and updated (New York: Fireside, 2001). Other classics in relating include Robert M. Bramson's *Coping with Difficult People* (New York: Ballantine Books, 1981) and Melody Beattie's *Codependent No More* (New York: Harper & Row, 1987). Be careful though: there's a lot of trash out there! Generally speaking, if the cover seems to promise you unending wealth, glory, and better sex, that's not a resource a minister wants to add to his or her professional skills shelf! From a more technical perspective, we should read widely on the general subject of pastoral care. I have already mentioned the writings of Wayne Oates as a good source. Many clergy testify that the work of Eugene Peterson has been tremendously helpful to them. See, for example, *Under the Unpredictable Plant: An Exploration in Vocational Holiness* (Grand Rapids: Eerdmans, 1982).

> Thomas Merton taught me something important about getting the most from my reading. He kept personal journals. Many times he wrote about what he was reading, in a dialogue with the material that was both intellectual and personal. In my own experience, such a practice helps me identify and appropriate useful counsel from all kinds of reading, including the books noted here. MAS

The primary suggestion I wish to make here, though, comes from my own experience. After 15 years as a pastor, I took my first course in clinical pastoral education. Many seminaries or denominations now require or encourage such a course as part of the basic ministerial degree, but mine did not. Many Christian counseling centers and seminaries, especially in larger cities, now offer CPE courses for those in parish ministry. For details contact the Association for Clinical Pastoral Education at *www.acpe.edu.* In such a course, you work with a cohort of other ministers and a supervisor to analyze your handling of actual pastoral interactions from your own ministry. Your peers and your supervisor work to help you challenge and refine your conversational techniques. The CPE process allowed me to examine my own interpersonal functioning with a depth and clarity I had not previously experienced. For any pastor who works with people, I recommend CPE.

Note, though, that it's important to discover the philosophy of the specific CPE program in which you wish to participate. In earlier years, some CPE supervisors thought it was their duty to create an atmosphere in which students were critiqued harshly indeed. Many experienced that approach as abusive. If you're considering a program, schedule an appointment with your potential supervisor and ask how he or she approaches the process.

A lifelong commitment to increasing our own self-awareness of how we conduct ourselves in relationships is the key to increasing competence in interpersonal skills. If you're having trouble in a particular area and you can't find written resources to help you, or if the issue keeps coming up, remember what we have said before about counseling. It's always better to seek advice from someone you trust than to let a problem fester. Some psychologists form groups to deal with specific problems in relating to others.

One possible model for resource is the development of an ongoing peer consultation group. Such a group, in which several ministers work in concert with a pastoral counselor or therapist to deal with situations from their parishes on a continuing basis can be a valuable resource. JAH

If you have ongoing issues in this area, you might want to seek out such a group. Nobody expects those of us in the ministry to be perfect, but it's important for us to be ready and willing to address our own issues.

SEVEN

I Saw the Holy City

Competent Leadership

The occasion hadn't started out as a rump elders' meeting for Third Church, but somehow it had ended up that way. When they began the regular monthly last-Friday potluck 15 years ago, all three couples had been part of the young adults' Bible study at Third Church, and none of them had been an elder. Now Sheila Van Kamp was chair of the board, Rodney Thorson was serving his second term as a board member, and Ed Brown had just been elected. Not only that: each of their spouses had served in leadership positions at one time or another in their 250-member congregation.

Actually the pastor's leadership was the unofficial topic of tonight's agenda. Specifically, did Pastor Carlson have enough of it—and if not, why not?—and if not, how could he be encouraged to do better?

The simple truth was that things at Third Church weren't going all that well. Three years into the Carlson pastorate attendance was down, income had plateaued, and enthusiasm was flagging. It was becoming more difficult to get volunteers. The church seemed to lack direction, and Greg Carlson didn't seem to be doing anything about it. Meanwhile, Second Church across town was booming under its enthusiastic young pastor, and First Church downtown under its suave and statesmanlike leader was continuing its traditional role as the place for community movers and shakers.

"I just don't know," Ed observed after about 30 minutes. "I realize I'm new on the board, but it just seems to me that we're not getting anywhere. I heard last week that the Henleys are considering leaving the church. If we can't keep good families like that, we're in real trouble!"

"Maybe it's time for a change," Rodney said. "In my business, if a salesperson can't perform, they're out. Shouldn't the church operate like a well-run business?"

"I don't know," Sheila demurred. "Greg is a really good person. The children and the older adults love him. And he's the best preacher we've had in 15 years. Shouldn't we be looking for ways to encourage him to be a stronger leader?"

"Leaders are born, not made," Rodney argued. "And Greg is just not a leader. We can't afford to waste the next five years trying to help him become one."

Such discussions tend to be interminable, so we'll leave our Third Church friends at this point and ask a few questions ourselves. Just what is competent pastoral leadership? If you don't have the skills to do it, can you acquire them? And, if so, how?

The Alban Institute has identified leadership as the single most crucial issue in the American church as we enter the twenty-first century.[1] In the Institute's special report on the issue the researchers talk about the declining numbers and quality of clergy in the mainline churches, the special challenges facing women clergy, and the ferment that seems to be creating a new paradigm for clergy and lay leaders in many denominations.

Certainly they're right about the centrality of the issue. A simple search under "leadership" in my own seminary's small library revealed more than 400 books on leadership, many of them with such titles as *The 108 Skills of Natural Born Leaders, The 21 Indispensable Qualities of a Leader,* and *30 Days to Competent Leadership.* Ministers want to be good leaders. They're frightened that they won't be. And they're looking for help wherever they can find it.

The class of senior seminarians whose self-assessments I reviewed for this book talk a lot about how to be a leader. They talk about the value of "servant leadership" as set forth by Jesus in the gospels. They talk about the desire to come alongside a congregation and help parishioners discover their own vision for ministry. They talk about their own reluctance to assert themselves in situations where pastoral authority is needed. Perhaps not surprisingly, the most experienced leaders in the class display the most comfort with their own identity as leaders and the least anxiety about asserting themselves appropriately when necessary. One student used a particularly apt image:

> A tugboat leads the ship out of the harbor safely. Although the ship could do its own thing, it trusts the tugboat to get it there safely. The power is all in the big ship, but it yields its power to the tugboat for direction. This is what a pastor is like. I believe pastors must realize the power the congregation has and be very respectful of that in order to be a good servant leader. That is how I would describe my style. I am a servant leader who realizes that I have been given the job of safely guiding the congregation out of the harbor in order that they may do ministry and do it to their full potential.[2]

From my own perspective, it's in the balance between servant-hood and self-assertion that leadership is found. *A Christian leader embodies Christlike qualities of servanthood and self-assertion that help a congregation both to remain faithful to its values and to move forward in its specific mission.* In this sense church leaders require a wide range of skills. For example, "We need someone who can run a fund-raising campaign and lead that recalcitrant board of deacons!" But leaders also require the more spiritual, character-based imagery being used by scholars such as Robert Clinton, associate professor of leadership at Fuller Seminary, whose writings have become influential in the "emerging leader" movement.[3] For example, "We need someone who loves Jesus and is being conformed to the image of Christ." Obviously we want all Christians to love Jesus and to be conformed to the image of Christ, but we expect our leaders to model this behavior for us.

I don't, however, view these differing approaches as either contradictory or mutually exclusive. A leader does need skills, and a leader does need good character. Churches in the new millennium desperately need ministers of character who are competent in the skills of leading a congregation.

Character in this context means the ability to embody and express the basic Christian virtues often described as the fruit of the Spirit: "love, joy, peace, patience, kindness, generosity, faithfulness, gentleness, and self-control" (Gal. 5:22-23). Paul gives a somewhat more behavioral, congregational description of the same virtues in Romans:

> Let love be genuine; hate what is evil, hold fast to what is good; love one another with mutual affection; outdo one another in showing honor. Do not lag in zeal, be ardent in spirit, serve the Lord. Rejoice in hope, be patient in suffering, persevere in prayer. Contribute to the needs of the saints; extend hospitality to strangers. Bless those who persecute you; bless and do not curse them. Rejoice with those who rejoice, weep with those who weep. Live in harmony with one another; do not be haughty, but associate with the lowly; do not claim to be wiser than you are. Do not repay anyone evil for evil, but take thought for what is noble in the sight of all. If it is possible, so far as it depends on you, live peaceably with all. Beloved, never avenge yourselves, but leave room for the wrath of God; for it is written, "Vengeance is mine, I will repay, says the Lord." No, "if your enemies are hungry, feed them; if they are thirsty, give them something to drink; for by doing this you will heap burning coals on their heads." Do not be overcome by evil, but overcome evil with good.
>
> Romans 12:9-21

From a character standpoint, being a pastoral leader means loving people one at a time for Jesus' sake. As I look back on my own years of pastoral ministry, I am proud of the things the churches got done. Far more than those measurable achievements, though, I cherish the people whose lives were touched or changed. Ultimately the kingdom of God is constructed not with bricks and mortar or even video screens but rather with one human heart at a time. A minister who loves people can learn to be a leader. A leader who doesn't love people is no minister.

Learning to be a leader, though, also requires acquiring specific skills. Among the skills needed are those of discerning a vision and setting goals, motivating others, negotiating difficult decisions, and assuming responsibility. Congregations need people who have a vision for ministry and who are willing to think and work outside the box of tradition to achieve that vision. Therefore, in the remainder of this chapter we will address learning to be a leader by looking at these four skills.

Discerning a Vision and Setting Goals

In many ways churches are like living organisms. They go through stages of birth, growth, maturity, decline, and death. No one wants a church to die, although some must do so for the greater good of the kingdom, and some must do so to be reborn to a healthier life.

In their book *Leading Congregational Change: A Practical Guide for the Transformational Journey,* church transformation consultants Jim Herrington, Mike Bonem, and James H. Furr write out of their work of revitalizing congregations within the Houston Baptist Association.[4] In their scheme, the discernment of vision is a key factor in leading a congregation to health, and the senior minister is the key player in discerning God's vision for the congregation. They do not suggest that he or she operates as a lone ranger in discerning and communicating God's vision to a congregation. Rather the pastor works with a "vision community" of trusted congregational leaders. The authors describe a process by which the pastor discerns God's vision, the vision community of lay leaders contribute their own discernment of the vision, and this merged vision from the pastor and the lay leaders is communicated to the congregation, whose members shape and adopt the vision as their own.[5]

Theirs, of course, is just one example of the dozens of models for vision casting now available. Some would argue that the process for casting a vision and adopting specific goals from that vision should be much more congregationally driven than these authors suggest. I cite their model, however, because they describe what I have repeatedly experienced in my own pastoral work. As pastor, it fell to me again and again to articulate a congregation's emerging vision.

I never entered a pastorate with the specific goal of changing a church. Nor (I hope) was I ever arrogant enough to believe that I and I alone knew what needed to happen for a congregation to move forward together under God. Nonetheless, I did enter every pastorate asking myself and the Lord the question, "What exactly is it that I am supposed to do here?" And in every case that question led me to some process of discerning a vision and setting goals for the church.

It's important to recognize the significant difference between discerning a vision for a church and setting goals for that congregation. Vision comes first and determines the goals you set. Searching for a vision, you ask such questions as, "What does God want this church's ministry in this community to be?" or "What is God calling this congregation to do and to be in this community?" or "To what mission and ministry is God calling this congregation?" Right now the vision for ministry of one church in our community is to reach educated 20-somethings. Another directs its ministry to those in recovery after addiction or divorce. Traditional congregations tend to have a much more generic sort of vision statement, such as "Reaching people and making disciples for Jesus Christ." They direct their ministry to the broader community rather than to a particular constituency.

The difficulty in vision casting is that congregations will often want to move directly to setting goals without first discerning their larger vision. If you don't know where you're going, you're not yet ready to decide how you plan to get there. A skillful leader will recognize that the time spent discerning, agreeing upon, and communicating a vision is essential to a congregation's long-term wellbeing. A congregation that knows where it is going is healthier, better focused, and better able to choose how to use its resources than a congregation that lacks a vision.

As Herrington, Bonem, and Furr describe it, the senior minister works with a vision community of church leaders to arrive at a tentative vision statement that is communicated to the church. A "vision statement" in this sense is a brief sentence summarizing as clearly as possible this congregation's mission in this community, however the congregation defines its community. The congregation then contributes its own input, and the whole community ratifies the vision together.

To be effective, the vision needs to be clear enough and engaging enough that any member can state it whenever asked. Once a vision statement is adopted, that statement is kept before the congregation in a variety of ways. Some congregations post the vision statement on the walls of the church. Others print it in the weekly bulletin. The pastor refers to it regularly in sermons. It is kept before the church finance committee as budget decisions are made and before the governing board as ministry directions are decided. The most important thing is that the vision be talked about, often and in many settings, so that it permeates the consciousness of the community.

The specific process will vary, of course, according to the congregation's tradition, polity, and situation. Some churches have a long-standing vision that seldom requires alteration. Others have never thought in these terms and will find the process difficult. Some may believe they just don't need any kind of stated vision. "We've done just fine without a vision here at First Church for the past 150 years. Why do we need one now?" I would argue, however, that vision casting is beneficial even if things are going well in a congregation. At the very least, stating your vision helps you understand why you are doing what you're doing. Others may discover that clarifying the congregation's vision helps members focus their resources and energy, resulting in more vigorous, effective ministry. Still others find that their vision needs to change radically to reflect their changing circumstances.

Whatever the case, it is only after a church's vision is clear that it is ready to move to the next step of setting strategic goals. In my own experience, the congregation is always full of ideas about what needs to be done next. Every interest group has its own agenda. The challenge lies in making certain all the various constituencies are heard, that each idea is consistent with the larger

In addition to large goals (the kind that take three to five years to accomplish), a pastor should help the church establish smaller, shorter-term goals that help measure progress toward the strategic goals. For example, one of my churches wanted to establish an ongoing ministry to children in a poverty zone. We broke the goal down into a set of steps: conduct a Bible school in the area and evaluate the response, recruit and train a certain number of volunteers, secure support from the identified leaders in the poverty zone, conduct a six-week program in the area and evaluate the response, secure a permanent site for the ministry, launch the ministry, evaluate the results after six months, and recommend further actions as needed, subject to annual review. This approach may sound impersonal, but in practice it provided numerous opportunities for involvement, meaningful measurements, and celebration. MAS

vision, and that the congregation as a whole is kept informed and given plenty of opportunity to buy into the process and its result.

Once a set of strategic goals has been developed, those goals should be used to set the congregation's agenda and budget for a period of approximately three to five years. Sometimes, of course, circumstances will change so radically that goals must be adjusted more quickly. Some planners recommend a yearly review. In today's society five years is a very long time for a goal to remain unchanged. The key is to make certain that specific goals remain in line with the church's vision. It's also important to remember, however, that churches change slowly and that a specific goal may take years to work its way into the fabric of church life.

The minister's role, once a set of goals has been developed, is to keep those goals before the congregation, and to help make it possible for the goals to be carried out. The minister's role is not to carry out the goals. Very often the mistake that clergy make is to identify themselves so closely with a congregation's goals that they lose their ministry and instead become de facto chair of the building committee or the education committee or the missions committee—or all three. I don't mean that you don't show up when the congregation spends Saturday working on the Habitat for Humanity project or when it's your congregation's turn to serve the meal at the homeless shelter. Your proper role as minister, however, remains the biblical one cited by the apostle Paul: "to equip the saints for the work of ministry" (Eph. 4:11). Your role is not to do the church's work yourself. Your role is to teach the church how to minister and then to encourage the members to do it. And that observation leads us logically to our next leadership skill.

Motivating Others

The ability to motivate others lies at the heart of competent leadership. When parish clergy talk about leadership, they most often mean motivation. "How do I get the people to do what they need to do?" Some pastors complain bitterly about their inability to persuade the congregation to take even the simplest initiative. Others say that folk seem ready and eager to do whatever needs to be done.

So is the problem of motivation a false issue? Are some congregations simply more active than others, regardless of what their pastor does or does not do? Or, is this an issue of charisma rather than character? We have all known ministers who seem somehow to have that magic touch. They speak, and people flock to hear them. They initiate a project, and the congregation rushes to carry it out. I don't believe, however, that we must simply accept a congregation's current level of motivation as fixed.

I believe there are significant differences between congregations, and I know to my sorrow (i.e., envy!) that some pastors do have more of that motivational gift than I do. But it seems to me that there are at least a couple of things anyone can learn about how to motivate a congregation to service.

First, it is often motivating to people to see you modeling initiative. When I went to my first little rural pastorate in the Kentucky bluegrass region, I was captivated by the fact that the church building possessed an old-fashioned belfry with a bell that could be rung by pulling on a rope. I envisioned ringing that bell every Sunday morning, calling the faithful to worship, and announcing our witness to the community. When I asked about it though, the story was a tale of discouragement. The bell hadn't been rung in years. "That bell keeps rusting, Pastor, and the roof is high and steep, and we can't get anybody to crawl up there and grease it." But I, being young and stupid, one Saturday morning early in my tenure, found myself up on that roof, crab-crawling my way to the belfry with a can of grease, while my wife stood 30 feet below on the ground holding a safety rope and muttering imprecations on the idiocy of husbands in general and me in particular.

I got it greased and, miracle of miracles, got down safely, but something far more important happened. A couple of church members passed by while I was up on the roof. And by the next day the new preacher's stunt was the talk of the congregation. Before church was over that morning, at least two members of the building and grounds committee made a point of saying, "You don't worry about that bell next time, Pastor. That's our job. You just tell us when you want it done." We rang the bell every Sunday for the rest of my tenure with that congregation.

The point is simple. Sometimes what a congregation needs is for you to model for them the things you want them to do. So if you want them to get involved, it is important to show up with your broom ready to sweep for the Habitat project, even if you can't drive a nail. And if you want them to tithe to the church, it's important both that you tithe yourself and that you let it be known that you do. To lead a church, you have to be willing to show by your own example exactly what you believe Christian service to be.

A second aspect of motivating others comes under the heading of encouragement. In the book of Acts, Barnabas, whose name means "son of encouragement," becomes the encourager for the young John Mark. He sees missionary potential in Mark, even after Paul has given up on the boy, and he saves Mark for the ministry by accompanying Mark himself on a mission trip. Less dramatically, pastors again and again come alongside those in their charge, encouraging people to undertake tasks that they may not be at all certain they can do.

It usually fell to me, as a Baptist pastor, to invite those whom the congregation had nominated to be deacons. In the churches I served, the deacons were the lay leaders of the church. They were expected to be spiritually mature, deeply committed both to Christ and to the work of the congregation. Very often people were astonished and frightened when I called to ask them to serve. I had to assure them repeatedly, "Yes, you can do this. No, you're not expected to be perfect." And, "Yes, I will be there for you if you get into trouble." In effect, what many people need is someone to see their potential, to give them an opportunity to serve, and to support them as they undertake the challenge. This is one of the most significant ongoing tasks of pastoral leaders. It's also important, of course, to develop in your congregation a culture of encouragement so that you're not the only one doing the encouraging!

A pastor needs to help the congregation develop the skill of discerning the talents and the potential talents of members and encouraging them as they develop those gifts. Many churches will use gifts surveys or some other written instrument to determine members' skills. Highly motivated people will often take hold and carry out a ministry if asked, with little or no input from you or anyone else. Many people, however, lack the self-confidence to risk a new venture unsupported. They need others to believe in them, to encourage them, and to walk beside them as they learn.

A third aspect of motivating others is even more closely connected to your character. That is your own consistent enthusiasm for the work of ministry. Some pastors are congenitally enthusiastic. Some become enthusiastic as their Christian life develops. Others have to work at developing their own enthusiasm and communicating enthusiasm to others. We talked in chapter 4 about the need to set your priorities and to husband your time. In writing this section, I assume that you're in effective control of your schedule. Even given that assumption, however, you can't overestimate the importance of communicating genuine, heartfelt enthusiasm as a motivating factor.

People want to believe that they are giving their time and energy to something important. For many people to believe that, they need to sense that their leaders believe in and are enthusiastic about what they are doing. Nothing communicates malaise to a congregation like a burned-out, uninvolved, unenthusiastic leader.

Ultimately, the only way to communicate enthusiasm is to have it. That means we must keep a close watch on our own health: physical, emotional, intellectual, social, vocational, and spiritual. All of these affect our ability to enjoy and to communicate enjoyment of what we are doing. If you find yourself becoming "blah" about your ministry, ask yourself why. Keep asking until you get some answers. And then change whatever needs to be changed to get your enthusiasm back.

Note that I am not talking here about maintaining some kind of cheerleading façade for the church. I am talking about believing and acting as though the work we are doing is the most important work in the world, because it is. If you believe that, your conviction will communicate itself to the church. They will believe and act that way, too. If you don't believe it, no leadership skill in the world will substitute for your unbelief.

Negotiating Difficult Decisions

In chapter 6 on interpersonal relationships, we talked about the importance of developing good skills for problem solving. All that I said in that section applies to the leadership skill of negotiating difficult decisions. Process is usually at least as important as product. Progress is often incremental. And you can never please everyone. In this section, however, I want to think more specifically about what a competent pastor does when the normal problem-solving process of the church isn't enough. There are at least two types of difficult decisions leaders need to negotiate: decisions you have to make *as a leader* and decisions in which you need to *be a leader.*

It's no secret that churches these days often face difficult, heart-wrenching decisions. "Do we move forward with our building project? What do we do with our staff in the face of declining income? Do we take a stand on a controversial issue?" These and dozens of other issues confront congregations every day. I'll use two examples from my own experience to communicate my perspective.

The first example comes from my second pastorate. It reflects a decision I had to make as a leader. The congregation, a church in northern California, badly needed to remodel and upgrade its building. While I was there, we hired an architect, developed plans, underwent a capital-funding campaign, and went through the difficult process of securing approval for the project from our upscale city's planning commission.

As we were getting close to obtaining approval, it became clear to me that my time with the congregation was nearing an end. The problem was that I came to this personal decision at about the same time I needed to make a pastoral decision about how aggressive to be in leading the church forward with the project. Should I push the members to go ahead, knowing that they might be without a pastor very soon? Or should I scale back my own advocacy of the project, and maybe miss the opportunity entirely?

My question was, "What constitutes responsible pastoral leadership in a situation such as this?" I'd seen so many pastors do this sort of thing badly. I'd seen them take a church deeply into debt and then leave. I'd seen them cease leading altogether for fear that they would make the wrong move. I'd seen them push hard for a commitment they had no intention of helping carry through. I didn't want to be that kind of leader. In our tradition, however, pastoral moves are usually negotiated secretly and not announced until negotiations are complete. One simply can't say, "Be careful about undertaking this project. I'm thinking about leaving next year." The experience of deciding how to proceed as a leader who might not be around very long taught me several things.

First, it is difficult if not impossible to lead when your personal goals and the goals of the church are in conflict. A wise minister will seek to align herself with a congregation whose vision and goals she can wholeheartedly support. Concomitantly, ministry is strengthened by a long-term relationship. Had I seen myself in that congregation for the foreseeable future, I would have had a much more positive approach to the project. When you're personally invested in a congregation's future, your goals and the congregation's goals are both compatible and complementary.

Second, a competent minister will nonetheless keep a clear boundary between ministry and projects. *People first* As ministers we must never lose sight of our ministry in our enthusiasm for a particular project. Ultimately, our responsibility is to help the church live out its vision. Our primary work is with people, not projects. If a project fails but the members of the congregation grow in their Christian understanding and service, we may have succeeded in the more important venture of ministry. As a leader, the process of equipping the saints goes forward whether a specific project goes forward or not.

The questions are "How is God leading the church?" and "How can you support that leading?" The more I thought and prayed about my dilemma in leading that renovation project, the clearer it became to me that the church both wanted and needed to do it, whether I was their minister or not. In a number of ways the long-term ministry of that congregation in that community hinged upon its ability to provide a more attractive and usable facility. As the rationale for the project became clearer in my own mind, I felt much easier about my role in promoting it as long as I was pastor. I was able to be enthusiastic about the project, even though I knew I might not be there to see it through.

Third, a competent leader in a volunteer organization makes certain the volunteers themselves are doing the work. The closer I got to the point of leaving, the more I realized that every aspect of the project needed to be in the hands of the congregation's lay leaders if they were to succeed when I was gone. It became increasingly clear to me that a leader does not strengthen lay leaders and members by doing things for them. You strengthen them only by helping them take responsibility for what needs to be done. You work through the congregation's committees. You decline to do things others can do. You empower the laity to take charge. By doing so, you enable them to go forward whether you are present or not.

This first example has been about how to make a difficult decision as the leader of a congregation. In the second example, I want to focus more on the decision to be a leader when the congregation is making a difficult decision. This second example took place in my last pastorate before coming to the seminary and requires a bit of explanation. The church had been a flagship congregation in its denomination for many years but had found itself increasingly out of sympathy with the denominational leaders over a number of issues, particularly the direction of the neighboring seminary and the place of women in congregational leadership. We had been in the forefront of the struggle to ordain women to the senior pastorate. The denomination was increasingly opposed to that practice.

In Baptist tradition, each congregation is autonomously governed and maintains denominational relationships voluntarily, if at all. While I was there, however, the Baptist group with which we had been traditionally allied issued a new confession of faith specifically excluding women from the senior pastorate. They also let it be known that all denominational schools and employees would be expected to support the new position. For me personally, the confession was the last straw. I knew that I could no longer in good conscience consider myself a part of that group, even as "loyal opposition."

My personal conviction, however, created an enormous dilemma for me as pastor of the church. I knew that the vast majority of the congregation agreed with me, but I also knew that the ties binding us to that affiliation were very strong indeed. A few older members were emotionally unable to contemplate a change in their lifelong loyalties. Some continued their support of the denomination's mission programs. One member was an employee of a denominational agency whose job required membership in a church of that denomination. Everyone was sensitive to the emotional hardship a decision in any direction might impose on others, but many of us felt that something had to be done to reflect the church's stand on key issues. The question I had to answer was how actively I should push the congregation for a decision.

Ultimately I elected to use the most powerful pastoral tool at my disposal. I chose to preach a well-advertised sermon on the subject, laying out my own convictions and position. I said to the church, in effect, "You must choose what you will do. For myself, I can no longer identify with and support this group. I consider it a matter of the integrity of my Christian witness."

I preached the sermon in late May. The summer was spent in endless discussion within the congregation about the best course of action to take. We held congregational meetings. I made myself available to anyone who wanted to discuss the issue with me. We encouraged those who did not want to speak in public to write out their opinions and send them to the church leadership. On the first Sunday in October of that year the church voted overwhelmingly to cease participating in or identifying with that denomination, but to allow individual members who wished to contribute to the work of the denomination to continue to do so through our church. Because of a technicality in the denomination's polity, the latter provision protected our member who was employed by a denominational agency and made allowances for those who could not emotionally make the break. What did all this teach me about leadership? Again, I learned a great deal.

I learned first that a pastor must sometimes take a stand. Sometimes you have to be a leader. For a Christian, some things are nonnegotiable matters of right and wrong. The specifics might vary for each of us, but when you get to a matter that is essential to your understanding of the faith, you must act in accordance with your conscience. Others may well disagree with you, and that will mean you have to help the congregation through the difficult process of deciding what to do. In effect, your decision to lead sets in motion the congregation's difficult decision.

Unfortunately that means, second, that you will inevitably damage your relationship with some members of the church. People who are Christians of good will can disagree on an astonishing variety of specifics about what being a Christian means. When you align yourself against the position some members hold, they may not be able to distinguish between you and your position on the issue. Your job is to keep talking with them, to let them know you still care about them, and to model how to disagree gracefully.

Third, the church must ultimately decide. In a congregational polity, that means the local church. In more connectional polities, it may mean the regional or national body. In any polity, however, once a decision is made, the individual minister is called to obedience to the congregation's or larger church's decision. You may not agree in every particular, but you must obey. If you cannot obey, then you must be willing to do what is necessary to be faithful in your own understanding. In effect, you have a difficult personal decision to make. You have to decide whether the issue or your relationship to the congregation or denomination is more important for you as a Christian.

Fourth, process is key, especially when difficult decisions must be made. A competent leader makes certain that the decision-making process is as fair as possible to all sides of the debate, and that it is perceived to be fair. If the leaders of the opposition can be identified, you may want to consult them as you construct your process for making the decision. As noted above, after my initial sermon, we did our best to make certain that there was ample opportunity for every constituency within the church to be heard throughout that summer and fall. As much as was humanly possible, we gave everybody the chance both to be heard and to feel that they could be heard.

Finally, the real leader of the church must be the Holy Spirit. We bathed our process in prayer. In late summer, there was a crucial meeting of the governing board, a body of about 40 people representing virtually every shade of opinion within the congregation. The board's task in that meeting was to give final shape to a recommendation that would go to the whole congregation for

I am familiar with the situation described here. Unfortunately, what followed the unity of the board meeting was a series of procedural moves by those in the congregation who feared losing control of the outcome of the debate. *Robert's Rules of Order* was used to cut off discussion prematurely. In the free church, at least, and I suspect in all churches, ministers need to maintain a healthy cynicism that takes account of all the possibilities for working mischief in a decision-making process. JAH

a final vote. The chair of the board requested prayer for that meeting weeks in advance. And in the meeting itself, every person was given the opportunity to speak his or her heart. We prayed again,

Don't jump the gun

and the recommendation passed unanimously. Given the deep divisions that had been evident throughout the process, the vote in that room on that day constituted what I believed to be a miracle.

My purpose in citing these two personal examples is certainly not to tout my own abilities to lead a congregation that needs to make difficult decisions. It's possible to disagree with my choices at any number of points in either of these scenarios, and a good many people did. Often I disagreed with myself. Instead, I hope to suggest something of the emotional difficulty and the inevitable struggle for integrity involved in being leader of a congregation. Neither the Scripture itself nor any denomination's governing documents give us explicit guidance on every decision that must be made. We often find ourselves groping through murky situations, searching for the best thing to do.

Ministry, in fact, is full of difficult decisions, small and large. To learn to negotiate those decisions with grace and integrity is the work of a lifetime. Like a kayaker running a whitewater rapid, you will encounter bumps and spills in ministry. But if you want to be a leader, leading through difficult decisions can and indeed must be done. And that leads us to our last major topic regarding competent leadership.

Assuming Responsibility

A leader is responsible—but not precisely in the way we think. Most of us subscribe to Harry Truman's "the buck stops here" school of leadership. In this way of thinking, which represents much of common wisdom in churches, whatever happens, good or bad, is ultimately the pastor's responsibility.

The leader is the person we get to blame. The participants in the potluck in this chapter's opening vignette believe that their church's lack of progress is somehow the pastor's fault. It may be, but that's not precisely the sense in which I think of responsibility. Instead, I believe that responsibility is a matter of the leader's character. In effect, "assuming responsibility" in this context means assuming responsibility for your own way of life.

A Christian leader must be a person of Christian character. In his relationship with the church, he needs to be constant in faithfulness, clear in his convictions, and careful in the way he lives out his own commitment to Christ. Bill Thrall, Bruce McNicol, and Ken McElrath, writers on Christian business leadership, explore the importance of this concept in their book *The Ascent of a Leader*.[6] They talk in terms of a "character ladder," by which they mean an individual's step-by-step progress in discovering and living out her own God-given potential. I commend their book to those who want to explore Christian character more deeply.

The question of taking responsibility for the way you live your Christian life is not new, of course. It goes back to the very beginnings of the church. When Paul is writing to the young pastor Timothy, advising Timothy on how to conduct himself in his ministry, he reminds his young friend to be true to his ordination: "For this reason I remind you to rekindle the gift that is in you through the laying on of my hands; for God did not give us a spirit of cowardice, but rather a spirit of power and of love and of self-discipline" (2 Tim. 1:6-7). In the compass of the concepts of power, love, and self-control we can find the boundaries of a competent leader's assumption of responsibility.

Power in the Christian life means the spiritual assurance and energy that come directly from the Holy Spirit through our relationship with God. These are what make the Christian life and therefore Christian leadership possible. No one should attempt to be a Christian leader who is not cultivating daily touch with the Spirit of God. In this most basic way, Christian leadership comes out of our relationship with Christ. Christ helps you do what you need to do. In this sense, of course, any practicing Christian can also be a leader.

> A minister will need to learn to deal with a certain amount of loneliness as part of the requirement of being a leader. As the minister takes on the role of leader, she inevitably separates herself in some measure from those who follow. JAH

In the daily ups and downs of church life, a leader functions out of her own relationship with Christ. We don't know precisely the situation in the church Timothy led, but we can infer that one issue might have been his youth. Paul's counsel, essentially, is that it's not your age that matters; it's your relationship with Christ. One aspect of leadership that churches seek in their ministers is the authenticity that comes only from that relationship. It may seem that such a thing should go without saying in a Christian context.

The danger, however, is that in a skills-based approach to leadership we may lose sight of the fundamentals of Christian practice that are essential in a leader. Competent Christian leaders assume responsibility on the authority of their own walk with Christ. From that walk, they gain the power to lead.

True leaders assume responsibility for loving the people according to Christ's concept of *agape* love. *Agape,* as it is used in the New Testament, is not an emotion. It is active good will. It means, in effect, to will and to work for the well-being of the other.[7] For leaders, *agape* is a tough-minded determination to work for what is best for individuals and for the congregation as a whole. As I write this chapter, I've been in conversation with one of my students who has just helped negotiate the merger of two churches of his denomination in their small town. As you may imagine, any number of pitfalls were encountered along the way to that conclusion. It had been tried before and had not worked. One factor that led to its success this time around was the student pastor's simple conviction that the merger was the right thing to do for the future of the congregations' witness, and his willingness to pay attention to people's legitimate concerns at every step along the way.

> I had a friend in denominational leadership who worked with many situations of conflict. He used to say, "Stay the course, and stay in touch." Or perhaps those phrases are reversed—"Stay in touch but stay the course." JM

He loved them and wanted the best for them, and they could see it by the things he said and did. With that kind of leadership, a pastor may take a congregation down many a dark and dangerous path, and they will follow. Competent Christian leaders assume the responsibility of *agape* love.

The final aspect of Paul's admonition to Timothy about leadership calls us to self-discipline. I believe Paul means that Timothy should keep to the essentials of the faith amid opposition and distraction. Churches and those who write about leadership talk a great deal about the need for "servant leadership" after the model of Christ. They're right, of course, but too often that truth seems to get transmuted into a kind of doormat theology. A servant is seen as one who never sticks up for himself or herself but puts everyone else's needs first. Or, even more dangerously, a servant leader is seen as one who takes charge and wears herself out for the sake of the ministry.

I believe, however, that a true servant leader is one who remains a servant of Christ in every situation, one who has the self-discipline to keep to the essentials of the faith and to the purposes of the church, no matter what the difficulty or distraction. In this model, a minister will indeed be a servant of the church and will also be a servant of Christ who maintains a healthy sense of integrity and personal boundaries. He will know what he is about and why, and that internal clarity of purpose will inform the specifics of his ministry.

This kind of leader knows where the church is going, understands what needs to be done to get there, and focuses personal energy on doing those things and not doing other things. One pastor I know of led his church to grow through divorce-recovery ministry. The congregation served a county where the percentage of divorced people was high. So the leaders concentrated on building a first-rate program for the divorced and their children. The congregation had all the needs any church has—staff members, a building, and a comprehensive program. Every other need, however, was measured against the requirements of that primary ministry. Competent leadership is disciplined leadership.

So does all this mean that a good leader is never blamed when things go wrong? Quite the contrary—those who lead through the power of the Spirit, the principle of *agape* love, and self-discipline will frequently be blamed for all kinds of mishaps. The point is rather that a leader who assumes responsibility for his or her own life and work under Christ will be capable of moving forward in both good times and bad. Out of her own relationship with Christ and her focus on caring for others will come the capacity to lead. We will almost inevitably be called on to lead at times when things don't go well, but whether things go well or not won't be the point. The point will be serving Christ and Christ's people.

Assessment

Clearly, discerning a vision and setting goals, motivating others, negotiating difficult decisions, and assuming responsibility are things that leaders do. Discerning how well you do them is another matter. It's important both to learn to assess our skills as leaders and to search for ways to improve. On the one hand, of course, suggesting further assessment of the leadership skills of people likely to read this book hardly seems necessary. As I mentioned in the beginning of this chapter, leadership is in many ways *the* issue in the American church in these early years of the twenty-first century. As such, leadership may well be the most-assessed characteristic of every parish pastor. Church people assess us as leaders continually, just as those in our opening vignette assessed their pastor. We assess ourselves. Our peers assess us. Our judicatory leaders assess us, and we assess them. Much of this assessment is informal, of course, but increasingly congregations and judicatories are moving toward more formal assessment models. The clergy self-help literature is perhaps more abundant on this issue than on any other. The Christian journal *Leadership* deals quarterly with topics related to the issue. For many of us, however, all this attention merely means that our anxiety about our competence in leadership is higher than it once was for those in our profession, but we still do not know anything specific we can do to become better leaders.

For those who would like to explore further their own potential for and patterns of leadership, however, one of the most helpful tools toward self-understanding, *Profiles of Ministry*, was developed by the Association of Theological Schools, the accrediting agency for seminaries and divinity schools in the United States and Canada. The *Profiles of Ministry* assessment is often given to master of divinity students. It's designed to help individuals understand their own style and approach to ministry. By presenting a person with a number of case studies, each with several possible solutions, the test measures what one is most likely to do in a variety of leadership situations. Seminaries use the test to help students discover strengths in their ministry style that can be cultivated and weaknesses in their style that need to be addressed. It is also available to pastors, ministerial groups, and lay leadership groups in churches. If you want to think through your own approach to leadership, or if your congregation or group wants to understand how you can work better together, I recommend *Profiles of Ministry*. Note that the test must be administered and interpreted by someone who has been trained to do so. There is, of course, a fee for administration and interpretation. For further information log on to the Association of Theological Schools' Web site at www.ats.edu, or write to ATS at 10 Summit Park Drive, Pittsburgh, PA 15275.

You can also find a wealth of information in the literature on leadership I've alluded to in this chapter, as well as online or at a good theological library. Alban Institute titles that might be helpful include *Learning While Leading: Increasing Your Effectiveness in Ministry,* by Anita Farber-Robertson with Meredith Brook Handspicker and David Whiman; *Personality Type and Religious Leadership,* by Roy M. Oswald and Otto Kroeger; and *When Better Isn't Enough: Evaluation Tools for the 21st Century,* by Jill M. Hudson. Leading is difficult, and leading the church is a consistently challenging art. A competent minister will need to learn and grow continually as a leader. Good leaders never finish getting better. Good leaders lead by growing.

EIGHT

Abide in Me

Competent Spiritual Development

It was three o'clock on a Wednesday afternoon. Pastor Ed Johnson walked into the deserted sanctuary of Grace Church and sat down as near to the center of the room as the configuration of the pews would allow. Ed loved the sanctuary of Grace Church. He loved its old wood, its delicate arches, its elaborately carved proscenium over the choir loft, its massive gallery pipe organ, and the 1920s art-deco feel of its beautiful stained glass. On any ordinary day, he took solace just from walking into the room.

But this was no ordinary day. It felt normal enough externally. In the distance Ed could hear the piano lesson being taught by the minister of music in his basement studio. Somewhere a vacuum cleaner was whirring. The aroma of tonight's church-supper pot roast drifted lazily through the building. Things couldn't seem more mundane.

But Ed was in turmoil. He just wasn't sure he believed this stuff anymore. He wasn't quite sure how it had happened. Some time ago now he had realized that he didn't pray any longer except in his role as pastor. He read Scripture only to prepare a sermon. For a long time he'd accepted these realities as part of the normal disillusionment involved in being a religious functionary. When you prayed for a living, it was tough to want to pray on your own time.

Gradually though, his inner life, his real life, had moved further and further from the Christian ideal. He seldom prayed now. Worship failed to touch him. His sermons were academic and literary exercises. With the congregation, he felt more like a counselor than a pastor. He hadn't felt God's presence in so long that he wondered if he ever would again. This afternoon, quite suddenly, he'd begun to feel like such a hypocrite that he just didn't know whether he could do this even one day longer.

For the first time in months he found himself praying. "God, if you're up there at all, I need help!" he demanded. "What in the world am I going to do?"

Obviously, Ed is an extreme. Most of us are more in touch with our spiritual lives than Ed seems to be. Just as obviously, no one can measure or evaluate with certainty the state of another person's relationship with God. That kind of measuring takes place at a much higher level than authors of Alban Institute books are privy to! Spiritual growth doesn't take place in precisely the same way or on precisely the same schedule for any two individuals. Ministers, moreover, are expected to "be spiritual" as a matter of course, as part of the discipline of living under ordination. Some might argue that experiencing spiritual turmoil or uncertainty or needing to be told how to grow spiritually should in itself disqualify one for parish ministry.

The senior students in our seminary's Readiness for Ministry colloquium reflected all these conceptual ambiguities in their self-assessments of spiritual growth. They were challenged: "Evaluate your habits in the area of Bible study, prayer, evangelism, mentoring, concern for the marginalized, and stewardship. You may want to explore Christian virtues such as love, acceptance, forgiveness, patience, hospitality, etc." Substantial numbers of them chose to answer as though the categories were a simple checklist: "I read my Bible in the morning. I would like to pray more. Our family tithes." Interestingly, the students almost unanimously ignored the second sentence altogether. I think often we either don't know how to evaluate our own maturity in such matters or find it unseemly to do so. Reading their responses as a group, I couldn't escape the feeling that students at their level of training experience considerable discomfort with the concept of spiritual growth, as well as considerable uncertainty about its meaning. Much of that discomfort seems to relate to the simple fact that spiritual growth is not a skill as such. It is a state of being. Pastors too may feel uncomfortable here. We know how to evaluate whether our sermons are improving. We're less able to gauge our relationship with God.

Reading the self-assessments of the senior seminarians, however, I found that one or two responses were so different from the general run as to be noteworthy. One student offered his personal testimony. It read, in part:

> Finally I was forced to lay it all before God. If [professional ministry] is what he wanted me to do, then he had better come up with the finances to go to [college] full-time. Surrendering my will to his was the most difficult thing I think I have ever done. . . . The day before classes started my junior year I said I would go to become a pastor and changed my major to pre-sem and theology. The next day God swung the financial door open. . . . I have learned patience and humility through the four-year affair my father had. I learned that I cannot be his or anyone else's Holy Spirit. I cannot change things. I cannot fix things, and I cannot force things though I still may try a few times. I have seen answers to prayers that I wished I had not prayed for. I have had almost every toy there is and lost them. I have seen God change the most hardened wicked hearts to hearts of love and compassion. . . . I have had close friends and my father betray me. I have been threatened by the mafia, bribed by government officials, and conspired against. In all that mess I can truly say God has given me more than I could have imagined. I feel like the luckiest guy on earth.[1]

It is not the drama in this student's story that makes it noteworthy. I actually left out some of the more dramatic parts. It is the authenticity with which he relates his spiritual pilgrimage to his life situation. This student exhibited the authenticity sought by Ed in our opening vignette. And it is the quest for increasing spiritual authenticity, I believe, that should occupy the minister's personal pilgrimage. The great majority of us are not seeking to become more pious to mark our spiritual journeys. Rather, we seek to become more real. Ministers who are growing spiritually are ministers who are becoming more and more authentic, healthy, whole human beings in relationship with God. They are becoming the people they were meant to be.

To some extent, we have already dealt with essential aspects of this spiritual journey. In addressing issues of accountability, boundaries, and priorities a minister establishes the dimensions that make spiritual growth possible. No program or discipline, however, can ensure that you or I grow spiritually. Such growth comes only as we respond faithfully to the challenges of life. It's your own attitude that makes growth possible for you. Any suggestions I make about to how to grow spiritually must necessarily assume that the reader wants to do so and is willing to pursue a deeper relationship with God.

> The adage "Know thyself" means, among other things, "Know what you know and know what you don't know." Part of becoming a mature human being is learning to recognize both your strengths and your limitations. JAH

A single chapter in a book of this length can't possibly say all that needs to be said about a minister's spiritual growth. One might profitably use all the pages allotted for this chapter to provide an annotated bibliography of works on the spiritual disciplines. Nonetheless, having stated as clearly as possible that I can't do what I'm setting out to do, I shall now in a modest way attempt to do it.

The essentials of the Christian life form the building blocks of Christian spirituality in the same way that the five pillars of Islam form the essentials of spirituality in that faith. One difference between Islam and Christianity, however, is that there is no universal agreement on precisely what the Christian essentials are. For purposes of this book, I shall choose six aspects of Christian faith that our seminary faculty asks our students to assess in their Readiness for Ministry documents. We select these because they represent significant aspects of Christian culture in twenty-first century America. These essentials are prayer, Bible study, spiritual direction, evangelism, concern for the marginalized, and stewardship. A minister who is growing in these areas should increasingly embody what it means to be an authentic Christian person.

Prayer

Perhaps no other contemporary American writer has contributed as significantly to our understanding of prayer as Richard Foster. His books *Celebration of Discipline: The Path to Spiritual Growth* and

Prayer: Finding the Heart's True Home contribute both a method-
ology and an attitude toward prayer that should make these books
an essential part of any Christian's library.[2]

In *Prayer* Foster begins with these simple words: "To pray is to
change. This is a great grace. How good of God to provide a path
whereby our lives can be taken over by
love and joy and peace and patience and
kindness and goodness and faithfulness
and gentleness and self-control."[3] He
argues that the grace of God is in fact
big enough to welcome each of us, no
matter how blotted our copybook or
how tangled our emotions and motiva-
tions. If we simply take the step of moving toward God in prayer, God will
begin bit by bit to show us God's own
heart, and in the process to show us the
truth about ourselves.

Prayer, at its most basic, is talking
with God. Some of us do that awk-
wardly, some formally, more mindful of
distance than closeness. Some of us simply never make the time. Some of us fill

As I mentioned earlier, I swim
regularly as a way of staying healthy,
both physically and emotionally. At
the pool there is a stream of pennants stretched across the water.
Often I ascribe to each of the pennants the name of a person or an
issue or a congregational concern.
Then I pray for each as I move in
the water. This practice also helps
me concentrate on relationships or
issues that are frustrating. The effect of using exercise in combination with prayer often dissolves or
relieves the frustration. Some issues
require only a lap! Others, more. JM

our prayers with words, blocking whatever God might have to say
back to us. A minister who wishes to grow in prayer will, I think,
take a few basic steps.

① The first is that he or she will develop a regular routine of prayer.
Prayer takes time. Martin Luther famously held, "I have so much
business I cannot get it done unless I pray three hours every day."
Today's preachers would be hard pressed to find three hours in one
day for prayer, but you can find time if you are determined to do so.
As the pastor of a congregation, I tried to make my first half-hour in
the office a consistent time of prayer. Whatever time of day or loca-
tion you choose, it is crucial to choose a time and a routine to which
you can consistently be faithful. Prayer takes time.

② Second, growing in our prayer life requires thought and stimulation. It's important to read the best traditional and contemporary
works on prayer. In addition to Foster's works mentioned above,

classic volumes such as St. John of the Cross's *Dark Night of the Soul,* Blaise Pascal's *Pensées,* Brother Lawrence's *The Practice of the Presence of God,* and George Buttrick's *Prayer* offer us perspectives on prayer that stretch our imaginations and cause us to consider prayer in helpful new ways. By reading about how others have engaged in and been changed by prayer, we open greater possibilities for God to shape our own lives through prayer.

③   Third, then, to move forward in our daily relationship with God, we must enter into a constant process of surrender in which we allow God to change us. In this sense, prayer can't be limited to a single setting or time of day. It is more of an ongoing conversation. Perhaps the greatest barrier to spiritual growth through prayer is that most of us, clergy or not, don't really expect anything to happen, and we certainly do not expect to be changed by it. We approach our daily office or construct our extemporaneous petitions as a monologue rather than as a conversation. We give God no opportunity to respond, and as a result we hear little or nothing of what God may be eager to say to us. There are other barriers, of course. In my own life, the most significant barrier to meaningful prayer has been those favorite sins to which I stubbornly cling and that keep me from surrendering to God's formative purposes in my life. Too often God does not speak to me because I am not willing to hear. I am more committed to maintaining my spiritual status quo than to changing at the call of God. More than anything else, it is the cultivation of an expectant attitude of ongoing conversation that allows God's Spirit the opportunity to speak to our own spirit through prayer.

When I was a lay professional and intern, I was quite self-conscious about praying aloud. My intern supervisor urged me to just do it— pray aloud, and it will become natural. I did. The unease disappeared, and I find I'm able to be open when I pray aloud. There are times when the expressions surprise me. The Holy Spirit is at work. JM

A competent minister will make a dogged and determined effort to be faithful and diligent in prayer. He or she will do this not because it is a minister's job, but because prayer is the primary way for a believer to cultivate a personal relationship with God.

Bible Study

The second significant avenue for spiritual growth for clergy is Bible study. Bible study, in the sense I mean, tends to be even more neglected than prayer precisely because parish clergy spend so much of their time studying the Scripture to prepare for sermons and lessons and therefore think they have the practice covered. As a function of the limitations of time and energy, many ministers read the Bible only as part of our jobs. We encourage laypeople to read Scripture devotionally, but we put most of our own effort into exegetical study and research. Many good things, of course, happen during that process, but sermon preparation is directed primarily toward the congregation.

Bible study is always useful. The sense in which I want to highlight Bible study, though, is its usefulness as a tool for personal devotion and personal growth. The problem for ministers from a spiritual standpoint is that exegetical study and research tend to hold us at arm's length from the power of Scripture itself to speak directly to our own lives. Reading Scripture for what it has to say to me rather than for what it has to say to the church puts my life under the scrutiny of the living Word. One has only to hear stories like Augustine's conversion by hearing a portion of the book of Romans to realize that potential power.

In some years I have used an annotated Bible for my nightly devotions. The Spiritual Formation Bible has sidebars throughout the texts that cause me to reflect on what I've read in the texts. JM

So how does one grow spiritually by reading the Bible? You build time for devotional Bible reading into your schedule. Just as you set aside a portion of the day for prayer, so also you set aside time for reading Scripture for your own edification. That does not mean that you forget everything you learned in seminary about biblical interpretation. Indeed, it's a good idea to keep a commentary or biblical introduction handy for reference. The more adventurous among us may prefer revisionist volumes such as Marcus Borg's *Reading the Bible Again for the First Time*.[4] But the point of this kind of Bible reading is not to achieve perfect interpretation.

The point is to allow the Scripture itself to speak to your spirit. Some people read in what is called *lectio continua*. They begin at Genesis and read through Revelation. Some choose a single book or a genre of biblical literature and seek to absorb the meaning of the text. *The Book of Common Prayer* provides a continuous cycle of the Psalms, with selections for each day of the month. Any number of sources divide the Scriptures into readings that allow one to read the whole Bible in a year.

Scripture reading in this sense is itself a kind of prayer. You approach your reading in an attitude of acknowledgement that God's Spirit speaks to us through the words of Scripture. This expectation that God will speak through Scripture is neither magic nor superstition. It is a recognition of the revelatory power of God's Spirit through human words. Many of us are in fact in the ministry because the words of Scripture have at some point spoken to us in a particularly powerful way. Putting ourselves in a posture that allows Scripture continually to change us simply continues that conversion process.

Spiritual Direction

DANGER! One of the biggest dangers to the health of the church of Jesus is the minister who functions as a spiritual lone ranger. Yet relatively few ministers avail themselves after seminary of the opportunity for ongoing spiritual mentoring or spiritual direction in any kind of disciplined fashion. The practice of spiritual direction as such comes out of Roman Catholicism but has found appreciative audiences in recent years in some of the mainline Protestant communions and in some of the more charismatic branches of evangelicalism.

Definition Fundamentally, spiritual direction involves meeting on a regular basis with a ministerial colleague who serves as a kind of confessor, mentor, and counselor. Spiritual direction is not psychological counseling as such. Rather it is a relationship that seeks to foster spiritual growth by spiritual means—prayer, retreats, fasting, and other spiritual disciplines, as well as by searching for the working of God in one's own life.

Ed in our opening vignette obviously had a number of quite serious spiritual issues. He probably needed counseling by a qualified Christian psychologist to understand why he had allowed his relationship with God to become so disengaged. He seems to be out of touch with his own feelings. A significant portion of his issues, however, may have arisen from his allowing himself to operate without some kind of meaningful spiritual accountability. A spiritual director would almost certainly not allow a client to go on as Ed has done without at least drawing attention to his spiritual practices.

Spiritual direction has become a separate master's-level emphasis in many seminary programs around the country, and growing numbers of people make their living specifically as spiritual directors. While I recommend seeking such guidance, I also recognize that many clergy may not feel comfortable in such a relationship and that those in more connectional traditions may feel they already have too many people paying attention to their spirituality.

The real value in spiritual direction comes only when you trust the one who is offering the direction and are content to place yourself under his or her care. Accordingly, I want to offer three less formal alternatives for obtaining spiritual direction that I have found to be useful in my own life. My only caveat in so doing is to remind the reader that I am not thereby suggesting that spiritual direction is somehow unimportant to spiritual growth. Rather, because I believe it is so essential, I wish to suggest as many avenues as possible by which excellent spiritual direction may be obtained.

The first alternative is a spiritual friendship with someone senior to you in the faith. Serendipitously, throughout our years in ministry my wife and I have tended to gravitate toward friendships with couples a generation or two older than we are. One of the most meaningful of those friendships was with a retired minister and his wife who had served pastorates in our denomination for half a century. For several years, until the relationship was altered by her death, we found the two of them to be ideal spiritual counselors for us. They were intelligent, deeply Christian, and highly pragmatic in their approach. Over dinner we could discuss issues from our own ministry and benefit from their wisdom in a powerful way. Several things we learned in that relationship have become enduring aphorisms for our own journey. You can't *make* such a relationship happen, of course. Either you click with someone or you don't. Our good fortune of enjoying several such relationships across the years, however, suggests that such a thing is indeed possible. Note that relationships such as this lack the sort of formalized structure of accountability that characterizes true spiritual direction.

A second form of spiritual direction is a mutual confessional relationship with a ministerial peer. From the time we left seminary, I have developed one particular friendship with a peer who is a colleague in ministry. By letter, conversation, e-mail, and occasional face-to-face meetings, we have built a friendship in which we share much of our lives with one another. I would not hesitate to trust my friend with virtually any issue in my spiritual life. His willingness to be honest, direct, and caringly confrontational has become one of the most significant spiritual resources I have. In her new book *A Praying Congregation: The Art of Teaching Spiritual Practice,* Jane Vennard suggests this kind of mutually accountable "soul friendship" as a strong alternative to classical spiritual direction.[5] It's important to note that Vennard suggests a certain formality of structure in this kind of relationship. She wants the two of you as you begin to state clearly your expectations of one another and to set guidelines for the relationship. How often will you meet and what form will your conversations take? Will you take turns sharing and listening during a single conversation? Or will you alternate roles in separate sessions?

A third form of spiritual direction I have experienced is like a mixture of the other two. Those of us in pastoral ministry find ourselves working a good bit with those who are themselves trained in psychology or pastoral counseling. People in those branches of the ministry tend to apply their skills to their friendship relationships as well as to their professional ones. Some ministers find that annoying because they don't want to feel as though they are being constantly analyzed by their friend, but I have always found it to be extremely helpful. If you make such a friend, his or her skills of analysis and clarification can contribute enormously to your spiritual journey. In fact, this sort of mentoring is often most helpful to us precisely because we are better able to listen within the atmosphere of mutual caring such a relationship entails. Again, following Vennard, you will want to make sure that the two of you talk about the nature of your friendship and that the other party desires a mutual relationship in which each can benefit from the other's gifts. If you treat this like getting free medical advice from a friend who's a doctor, mutuality and accountability become simply taking advantage of a friend. Also, it's not necessary that your "soul friend" have any kind of special training at all. Any spiritually mature Christian could be a candidate for this kind of mutual relationship.

The goal of this kind of relational spiritual direction is to build accountability and guidance into the structure of the minister's life. Committed soul friendships add a depth and honesty to our Christian walk that come in few other ways. For those who are ready to seek a more formal relationship, however, resources are considerable and growing. A simple search under "spiritual direction" on the Internet will produce many organizations and individuals who practice spiritual direction. For books that will help you explore the issue before taking the plunge, consider Jeannette A. Bakke's *Holy Invitations: Exploring Spiritual Direction,* or Keith R. Anderson and Randy D. Reese's *Spiritual Mentoring: A Guide for Seeking and Giving Direction.*[6] Bakke writes from a more mainline perspective while Anderson and Reese take a more evangelical point of view.

Evangelism

In the tradition in which I grew up, the word "evangelism" carried a specific and emotionally charged meaning. It meant, specifically, the individual's responsibility for telling others the story of what salvation through Jesus Christ means and for encouraging them to accept that salvation for themselves. Because a similar definition has been used by a number of traditions, evangelism is a problematic word for many in American Protestantism. Our culture of individualism works against the idea of attempting to persuade others to alter their religion. Even for those graduating from seminary, to suggest that one's spiritual growth is somehow measured by one's competence in evangelism is likely to raise more than one or two defensive and theological hackles.

Perhaps it's better, therefore, to recast the discussion in slightly different terms. In his book *Testimony: Talking Ourselves into Being Christian,* the Presbyterian preacher and homiletician Tom Long speaks in terms of "testimony," by which he means the preacher's ability to function as a heartfelt witness, a joyous personal advocate of the Christ-way in life.[7] For Long, this kind of advocacy takes place primarily as we tell the stories of our own and others' individual journeys of faith. Such stories are not, or rather are only in the smallest part, about the initial beginnings of one's Christian pilgrimage. They are rather celebrations of the ways in which we discover our faith to be reliable and satisfying both in the crises and in the dailiness of life.

So what does it mean to think about growth in testimony as a measure of spiritual growth? A minister is a practitioner of the Christian faith. We serve because we believe the way of life we have chosen in following Jesus is superior. With the most profound respect for other traditions, other choices, and other convictions, we still believe the way of Christ reflects humankind's most direct and unambiguous path to relationship with God. Many of us would make this affirmation much more strongly than that.

To grow in testimony, then, is to move in precisely the opposite direction as Ed in our opening vignette. It is to move toward more joy, more gratitude, a more profound sense of the truth of the faith and of its power in every area of life. This deepening conviction should come neither from some kind of false expectation that the minister must act as a cheerleader nor from a sense of obligation to notch one's gun with converts, but rather from a growing sense of wonder as each step in our journey reveals new confirmation of the truth to which we have given ourselves. "Conversion, regeneration, mystical union, *metanoia*," so William Willimon writes, "are all attempts to speak of this turning of heart, body, and mind toward God—a turning that is occasioned by God's prior turning toward us in Christ. . . . Only a lifetime of turnings, of fits and starts, of divine dislodgment and detoxification, can produce what God has in mind for us. Daily we turn. Daily we are to take up the cross and follow. Daily we keep being incorporated into the Body of Christ that makes us more than we could have been if we had been left to our own devices."[8]

The suggestion that spiritual growth is measured by moving toward a joyous sense of certainty in our faith does not, however, mean that such a movement is unimpeded. As Willimon states above, the Christian life involves daily recommitment. Christian Scripture, tradition, and hymnody are full of tales of the difficulties and dangers of the Christian way. Sometimes those tales are romanticized, but I don't mean that we should get swept up into some kind of ecstatic mysticism that loses touch with reality. True spiritual growth in your testimony is much more mundane. Simply put, it's the growing, joyous certainty that "this way of life works for me, and I wish everybody could have what I have." Such growth is dependent on our circumstances and our personalities. For some the ministry is such a hard life that joy is in short supply. Others seem to be hardwired to see God's grace in every trial. One's growth in telling the "good news" may be quite subtle. It may need to be measured in decades rather than in months or in years. Its absence over time, however, is an indication of spiritual anemia.

Does this mean that a minister doesn't need to be a "soul winner"? Quite the contrary, a minister must first of all be one whose own soul is being won by Christ, and who, in consequence, is more and more eager to assist in the winning of others. "Evangelism" as such is a specific spiritual gift, as we see in Ephesians 4:11. Not even every member of the clergy has it. Spiritual growth in this area does not mean that God is going to change our personalities. But every Christian, with the apostle Peter, is called upon to be ready and eager to give "an accounting for the hope that is in you" (1 Pet. 3:15). The more we grow comfortable and assured in our own Christian walk, the better able we grow to find ways to give that accounting that harmonize with our own strengths and spiritual gifts.

Concern for the Marginalized

In the story of the Judgment of the Nations in Matthew 25, Jesus gives the criteria by which the Lord will determine our eternal fate. Those criteria have nothing to do with theology, church membership, or even spirituality as it is traditionally defined. On the other hand they have everything to do with kindness: "I was hungry and you gave me food. I was thirsty and you gave me something to drink. I was a stranger and you welcomed me. I was naked and you gave me clothing.

It's important to emphasize that paying attention to the marginalized means recognizing and valuing the diversity of human life. Diversity includes the whole range of race, class, orientation, and culture—in other words, everybody! JAH

I was sick and you took care of me. I was in prison and you visited me" (Matt. 25:35-36). In effect, Jesus makes social ministry the single criterion of righteousness worthy of salvation.

That story should, I would argue, give serious pause to church members and clergy everywhere. At the very least it suggests that competent spiritual growth will include growing concern for and aid of the marginalized, and conversely it suggests that those who are not involved in helping the marginalized are therefore not growing spiritually.

Such an inference is, of course, quite controversial. In a famous exchange with a layperson, the Trappist monk Thomas Merton was once asked how he could spend his life cloistered in the Abbey of Gethsemane while there was so much need in the world outside. Merton is reputed to have answered, "The difference between you and me, Madam, is that I believe in prayer."

Most parish clergy, I suspect, if they are being honest, will say that there is a sense in which ministerial life militates against precisely the kind of concern for the marginalized that Jesus holds to be so crucial. Much of a minister's life is bound up in serving and preserving the institution of the church. You prepare and lead worship. You prepare and lead Bible studies and catechism classes. You worry about church organizations, church finances, members' health, maintenance of the facilities, membership recruitment, and a thousand other details. In many ways you become a creature of the institution, caring for and meeting the needs of the church people first. In many churches such institutional maintenance leaves little time or energy for reaching out to those on the edges of society.

It's useful to think of the minister's spiritual pilgrimage in terms of the categories of theological approach depicted in H. Richard Niebuhr's classic *Christ and Culture*. Niebuhr talks about the Christ of culture, Christ above culture, Christ against culture, Christ and culture in paradox, and Christ transforming culture. Many of us move through one or more of these categories in the course of our personal journey of faith. JAH

Indeed, in many areas, those on the edges of society are in fact the ones the churches and their ministers are least likely to care for or encounter. Christian churches are filled with "respectable" working-class and middle-class folk. The down-and-out, the addicted, the needy, the relationally broken, and the morally compromised are precisely the least likely to feel comfortable identifying with a Christian congregation. In effect, we church folk often tend ourselves to be uncomfortable with the marginalized, and consciously or unconsciously we fail to make them welcome. We grant them access to Christ's message of inclusion only if they first obey our unwritten rules of respectability.

Part of a minister's spiritual pilgrimage, then, involves working against the grain of American Christian culture. In the Midwestern city where I live, for example, there are at the moment two Christian divorce-recovery programs. One is Roman Catholic. The other is charismatic. The rest of the mainline and evangelical churches focus their efforts on marriage enrichment and the attempted rescue of marriages in trouble. They essentially ignore that huge percentage of the population whose marriages have already failed and who desperately need acceptance, healing, and help. Why? It's impossible to say definitively. My guess is that more conservative churches shy away from divorce-recovery ministry because they don't want to be perceived as somehow "approving" of divorce. Mainline congregations may not want to be perceived as judging those who are divorced. As a result they ignore one of the primary needs in American society and cut themselves off from ministry to a significant marginalized population.

A minister who is growing spiritually will be in the process of becoming increasingly sensitive to the needs of those on society's edges. He or she will be constantly on the lookout for legitimate needs in the community and for ways of meeting those needs. Christian ministry is ministry to "the least of these," or it is not ministry at all.

Many pastors grow into a meaningful commitment to social ministry by helping their church members do so. One of the most practical, sustainable programs for doing so is called "Operation InAsMuch." The goal is to provide church members with an opportunity to engage in hands-on ministries on a designated date. In my experience, up to one-half of a church's average morning worship attendees will participate. Church members get to break the ice, so to speak, and make connections with the poor and marginalized. An added benefit is that more and more church members choose to become involved in some ongoing social ministry. Check out www.operationinasmuch.com for detailed information. MAS

But how does all this social-ministry bias find its way into a chapter on the minister's spiritual growth? It is a mistake for the minister to view spirituality as somehow exclusively devotional and mystical. One might well become more spiritual by praying more. We should all pray more. Jesus' clear bias, though, seems to lie in the direction of providing hands-on help for those in need. That ministry might take many forms—direct assistance, advocacy, work for political or legal change, or consciousness-raising in your congregation.

One simple way to assess your growth in this area is to answer the following question. In the past six months what have you done in the name of Christ for someone outside your own family or church family? It's a sobering question. Spiritual self-examination usually is.

Stewardship

Stewardship can refer to any number of practices. In my earlier book on ministry,[9] I included an entire chapter on stewardship and dealt with the minister's family life, personal care, and time management under the stewardship rubric. Those matters are an essential part of the minister's self-discipline, but in this volume they are dealt with in other places.

Here I want to return to the first thing you thought of when you saw the word—money. It is entirely appropriate for a Christian minister to think first about stewardship of money because Jesus talked more about money, its dangers and its uses, than about any other single subject in all his teachings.

In American culture the ordained ministry has come to be one of the lowest-paying jobs that usually requires a graduate education. Congregations, in my experience at least, seem to suffer from profound ambivalence about their pastors' material well-being. On the one hand, they want to feel that they take good care of us. They want us to live in adequate housing and to dress appropriately for the congregation's socioeconomic level. On the other hand, they seem to resent ministers who live too well or project too much of an air of prosperity. There's a traditional aphorism in Baptist life in which the prayer of the congregation goes, "Lord, you keep the pastors humble, and we'll keep them poor!"

As a result, ministers and their families often struggle with the issue of stewardship. Churches in the tradition I come from tend to assume that their ministers give a full 10 percent of their salary to the church. While gifts to the church in most traditions are considered confidential, I as a pastor never cared to test that confidentiality by giving less.

The spiritual issue of stewardship for ministers, then, involves coping with the cultural and congregational expectations regarding your attitude toward money, while at the same time taking adequate care of your family, enjoying life, bearing witness to financial integrity in the larger community, and making reasonable provision for retirement. In his book *Money, Sex and Power: The Challenge of the Disciplined Life,*[10] Richard Foster argues that the Christian standard for stewardship, regardless of one's vocation, is simplicity. Foster makes the case that simplicity in the Christian's life means:

- Unity of heart and singleness of purpose.
- Joy in God's good creation.
- Contentment and trust.
- Freedom from covetousness.
- Modesty and temperance in all things.
- Grateful reception of material provision.
- Habit of using money without abusing money.
- Availability for kingdom purposes.
- Attitude of giving joyfully and generously.[11]

Acknowledging the dangers inherent in our human fascination with wealth, Foster thus seeks to help us keep our stewardship in Christian perspective.

While Foster comes from the evangelical/pietistic end of the American religious spectrum, it's useful to note that Yale professor Gaylord Noyce comes down in a very similar place in his chapter on money in *Pastoral Ethics: Professional Responsibilities of the Clergy.*[12] Even with the cultural changes that make younger clergy much less comfortable with the idea, Noyce says, "The Christian bias toward simplicity has a long and authoritative history."[13] Interestingly, Noyce ends his chapter on the subject with the admonition to the young pastor Timothy:

> Of course, there is great gain in godliness combined with contentment; for we brought nothing into the world, so that we can take nothing out of it; but if we have food and clothing, we will be

content with these. But those who want to be rich fall into tempta-
tion and are trapped by many senseless and harmful desires that plunge
people into ruin and destruction. For the love of money is a root of
all kinds of evil, and in their eagerness to be rich some have wan-
dered away from the faith and pierced themselves with many pains.

1 Timothy 6:6-10

Noyce is less prescriptive than Foster, but he comes to essentially the same place. Ministers need to get control of their attitude
toward money.

An important part of a minister's spiritual journey is therefore
cultivating an attitude that neither idolizes nor denies the good things
of this world. Getting your approach to the material things of life
right probably has as much to do with your long-term contentment
in ministry as any other single spiritual factor. If you want to become rich, chances are you're not going to be able to do that as a
pastor. When Foster suggests that "simplicity means availability,"
part of what he means is that you can't be free to do what God
wants if you're spending your time and energy worrying about money.

I mentioned in the first portion of this section that when I served
as a parish pastor, my wife and I tithed at least in part because we
knew that we were expected to do so. Something quite interesting
happened to me, though, as we continued that practice across the
years. I realized quite suddenly one day that we were being taken
care of. No matter what our needs, they always seemed to be met,
whether I thought we had enough money or not. I no longer "have"
to tithe because of a job that seems to require it. Nobody really cares
what a seminary professor gives. But my wife and I still tithe. What
I began doing out of obligation we continue out of joy. That is not
to suggest that by doing so we have all our spiritual priorities straight
with regard to money. But it is to say that this part of my own spiritual journey has proved more rewarding than I, at least, would ever
have dreamed.

Assessing Spiritual Development

How do you assess your spiritual development as a minister? In essence the issue is little different for clergy than for any other Chris-

tian. The only real difference is that we live out our spiritual lives publicly. In every other particular we are subject to the same processes of sin and grace, sanctification and backsliding as any other believer. The pilgrimage toward spiritual authenticity is lifelong and fraught with complications.

Perhaps the key elements here are a combination of awareness and perseverance. Ed's real problem in this chapter's opening vignette is that he stopped working on his own spiritual journey and then lost touch with the fact that he had done so. He simply stopped trying until he found himself so far away from the Christian path that he was no longer certain how to get back. Wherever we may be in our own relationship with the God of Jesus Christ, whatever specific issues we may encounter, a competent minister perseveres in his or her own intentional discipleship. Hence the writer adjures Timothy at the end of the section on money, "But as for you, [person] of God, shun all [love of money]; pursue righteousness, godliness, faith, love, endurance, gentleness. Fight the good fight of the faith; take hold of the eternal life, to which you were called and for which you made the good confession in the presence of many witnesses" (1 Tim. 6:11-12).

> In trying to practice consistent self-assessment, I've chosen to focus on a single key question: How am I doing at loving God without reservation and my neighbor as myself? I try to focus daily on the question. Bible study, stewardship, evangelism, prayer, ministry to the marginalized, and all the other topics addressed in this chapter find their place within my reflections. My working definition of a healthy Christian (lay or clergy) is that she or he is someone who is developing a deeper and wider love for God and neighbor. This kind of personal self-assessment does not take the place of friends or spiritual guides or more formal evaluations, but it helps keep me more nearly on track! MAS

If you find yourself in Ed's position, the first step toward spiritual health is to understand how you got there. It's important to tell your story to a Christian psychologist, spiritual director, or soul friend, whichever is most comfortable for you, and to listen to that individual's perspective. Sometimes others can see about us what we can't see at all about ourselves. The next step is to begin to make specific changes in your behavior. As you begin that conversation, consider the six areas of spiritual growth we've dealt with in this chapter:

Prayer

- How often am I engaging in direct, honest conversation with God?
- Am I allowing listening time in my prayers so that God can speak to me?
- Am I willing to hear God's answer?
- How can I structure my day to improve my practice of prayer?

Bible Study

- What's the latest spiritual insight I received from reading the Bible?
- Am I pursuing a plan for regular devotional Bible study?
- How can I make my personal study more informative and more interesting?

Spiritual Direction

- Is there anyone in my life who knows the truth about me?
- Do I have sufficient relationships with spiritual mentors or soul friends to keep me accountable for my spiritual journey?
- Am I reading regularly in materials that can strengthen my journey?[14]
- Am I willing to submit myself to spiritual guidance?

Evangelism

- Do I believe that I have the gift of evangelism?
- What is the essence of my own Christian story?
- Would I like to help others know what Christ offers believers?
- How am I making "telling the good news" compatible with my own Christian lifestyle?

Concern for the Marginalized

- Do I personally engage regularly in some form of Christian service for the needy?
- Have I shaped my personal behavior and political convictions according to Matthew 25?
- What group outside the church in my own community is most in need of my help?

Stewardship

- Am I living within my income? Paying my bills on time?
- Is tithing a joy for me? A burden? Not part of my Christian practice?
- Do I really believe that God takes care of responsible and generous Christians' material needs?
- What steps do I need to take to get my financial life on track?

Progress in spiritual growth is neither easy nor automatic. But the pursuit of spiritual growth is, I believe, a significant portion of what Christ means when he talks about the "narrow way." If we as ministers expect those we lead to follow the Christian path, we must first be willing to follow it ourselves.

I think it is very useful and helpful to have a pastor take at least one extra Sunday a year off to visit other congregations. One can be fed without feeling responsible for the service, and having a Sunday away is renewing to one's spirit. JM

For Further Reading

The following books were either used in the preparation of this chapter or referred to as additional resources. They are listed below for the reader's convenience:

Anderson, Keith R., and Randy Reese. *Spiritual Mentoring: A Guide for Seeking and Giving Direction.* Downers Grove, Ill.: Intervarsity Press, 1999.

Bakke, Jeannette A. *Holy Invitations: Exploring Spiritual Direction.* Grand Rapids: Baker Books, 2000.

Borg, Marcus J. *Reading the Bible Again for the First Time.* San Francisco: HarperSanFrancisco, 2001.

Foster, Richard J. *Celebration of Discipline: The Path to Spiritual Growth.* San Francisco: Harper & Row, 1978.

———. *Money, Sex and Power: The Challenge of the Disciplined Life*, San Francisco: Harper& Row, 1985.

———. *Prayer: Finding the Heart's True Home.* San Francisco: HarperSanFrancisco, 1992.

Long, Thomas G. *Testimony: Talking Ourselves into Being Christian.* San Francisco: Jossey-Bass, 2004.

Noyce, Gaylord. *Pastoral Ethics: Professional Responsibilities of the Clergy.* Nashville: Abingdon, 1988.

Sisk, Ronald D. *Surviving Ministry.* Macon, Ga.: Smyth & Helwys, 1997.

Vennard, Jane. *A Praying Congregation: The Art of Teaching Spiritual Practice.* Herndon, Va.: Alban Institute, 2005.

Willimon, William H. *Pastor: The Theology and Practice of Ordained Ministry.* Nashville: Abingdon, 2002.

The reader is also encouraged to explore the literature of Christian devotion, including such historical classics as *The Pilgrim's Progress* by John Bunyan and *Dark Night of the Soul* by St. John of the Cross.

NINE

House on the Rock

Competent Personal
and Professional Development

Pastor Erica Lundstrom strode into her office, closed the door a little too firmly, sat down behind her desk, and threw up her hands. She couldn't remember feeling more exasperated. Until today, she'd always enjoyed worship committee meetings, her bimonthly planning session with all those involved in worship leadership.

Today, though, Helen Johnson had thrown a wrench into the works. An advocate of innovation in worship, Helen wanted Erica to experiment with integrating video into her sermons. Helen was always talking about visiting her daughter, who attended the contemporary church in the city. Helen loved to see hymns, sermon outlines, and movie clips projected on the screen. She said they made worship at her daughter's church so interesting. For months she'd been dropping hints that Erica should try some of these ideas.

But today, she'd brought it up formally in the committee. "I'm convinced," Helen argued, "that we can do a better job of reaching and keeping our young people involved if we move our worship into the twenty-first century. Pastor Erica, why don't you try using a movie clip as part of your introduction to your sermon?"

Helen, of course, had no idea what she was asking. Erica knew very little about these newer approaches to homiletics, but she knew enough to know that she didn't know how to do it. Such things had never been dreamed of when she went to seminary back in the early days of VCRs. And now, in mid-career, she really didn't want to learn.

At heart, she had to admit to herself, Erica was a traditional-
ist. She liked the commentaries she'd bought as a student. She
liked the liturgy she grew up with. She liked the church's
established ministries. At the last pastors' retreat, when they'd
offered a session on that book about change, *Who Moved My
Cheese?*, Erica had ducked out for an afternoon of golf.

Maybe the truth was that she'd gotten a little lazy. Erica
knew that as a pastor she should be always learning, growing,
and seeking to move forward in her own understanding and
skills so that she could help the church move forward. But it was
so tough to find the time! She couldn't remember when she'd
last read a new book, much less taken a continuing-education
course or gone to a professional meeting. She'd given herself to
ministry, and, sure enough, ministry was taking all her time.

Calmer now, Erica stopped using her desk as a snare drum
and began seriously to think. "Maybe," she thought. "Maybe I
can find the time to take that new course on video in worship. I
don't have to like it to learn about it!"

Competence in ministry is a moving target. A ministry technique
that works in one parish may not work in another. What works today may not work five years from now. The Scripture never changes,
but understandings and interpretations of Scripture do change. The
joke when I attended seminary was that churches have to run as fast
as they can just to stay in the same place. You may not be a fan of the
specific innovation Erica struggled with. I could almost hear the
traditionalists (I am one!) groaning as I wrote. But conversations
like that one are taking place again and again in churches across the
country. The reality today seems to be that church leadership of any
kind requires constant adaptation, both personal and professional.
Definitions and paradigms of ministry are evolving rapidly as society
and the churches change more quickly than ever before.

I remember as a ministerial student asking a pastor in my home-
town how he kept up in his field amid the demands of ministry. I
received a dismissive reply: "I read so much in seminary I got sick of
it," he said. "I haven't done any serious reading since!" He'd been
out of seminary about 15 years at the time. As a professor 30 years
later looking back on that conversation, I can sympathize with that

pastor's impulse but not with its duration. Seminary is a lot of work. Students do get sick of being required to learn, and everybody deserves a break. But the demands of our field are such that none of us can afford to stop growing. Chapter 8 dealt with aspects of spiritual growth, which is certainly essential to effective ministry. But you can be quite mature spiritually and still not be a competent pastor. Competent ministry requires that we grow intellectually and professionally as well. What does that mean?

In the earlier chapters of this book we've dealt with a list of the understandings and skills essential for ministry and talked about ways of growing in each of those areas: understanding of your family of origin, self-motivation, communication skills, time management, stress management, interpersonal skills, leadership skills, and spiritual growth. In this final chapter we'll address two final tasks. First, we'll talk specifically about ways to grow intellectually and professionally as a pastor. Then, we'll address the issue of planning to grow in all the competencies we've discussed. How do you develop habits that nurture such growth? How do you seek out and experience opportunities for growth beyond your normal routine? How do you plan for long-term personal and professional development?

Making Growth a Habit

The days of ministry are full of surprises and demands. Every pastor knows how a phone call or an unexpected visit can alter all your plans and make an instant mess of your schedule. Despite the unpredictable nature of ministry, however, clergy need to set goals and priorities, to make plans and commitments, and to exercise discipline and reliability. We've talked in earlier chapters about the importance of taking time for such priorities as prayer, family, and yourself. As difficult as it might be to manage the many demands of ministry, though, we add one more component in this final chapter to the recipe for ministerial competence. That is the priority of growth.

Competent ministers are always growing. Our sample of senior seminarians knew that. They talked in glowing terms of their intention to do all the things after graduation that they hadn't had time to do in school—read, retreat, network, get involved with new ministries. What they almost universally failed to do, though, was to offer any specific plan for how they would integrate growth-related activities into their schedule.

Reading

To grow, you have to make growth a habit. For most of us, growth begins with reading. It's one thing to say that you will read new books to stretch your mind and enrich your ministry. It's quite another thing to take the hours from 2 p.m. to 4 p.m. every Tuesday to read. Everyone is different, of course, and the time you schedule for reading each week might not work for someone else. The crucial thing is to choose a time that works for you and stick with it.

Some like to relax with reading professional materials before bed. I find that, by that time of day, I'm tired and want something lighter. So I build in an hour for reading in late afternoon, because that seems to be a time when relatively little is going on and I can concentrate on what I'm doing. Others find that early morning is the best time for them. However you structure it, establishing regular weekly time for reading new professional material is an essential habit to cultivate if you want to keep growing.

The next question, of course, is "What do you read?" I suggest to my homiletics students that they read widely to enrich their preaching. Since preachers deal with scriptural interpretation, Christian history, evangelism, congregational practice, pastoral care, current events, and ethics, I suggest that preaching students read regularly in all these areas. It's also important to know what fiction is popular at the moment and to read it. In addition to what's popular, of course, we also need to read good writing and to pay attention to what makes it good. Do you know the name of the current U.S poet laureate, for example? Have you read anything he or she has written? Current writing can often provide some of the best sermon material as well as an insight into the kinds of issues with which church members are dealing. In addition, of course, a children's minister would need to be reading the latest materials in family and children's education. A youth minister should keep up in that area.

Sounds overwhelming, doesn't it? It need not be. Time is limited, and you can only do what you can do. If you keep one book going, read the newspaper, subscribe to a weekly newsmagazine, and take one or two professional journals, you should be able over time to add significantly to your professional knowledge. Two hints help to make such a strategy work. First, remember that your goal is growth over time. You're not studying for an assignment or cramming for a test. Ministry itself is the test. Second, you're under no obligation to finish every book or to put into practice every suggestion you encounter. Some things you begin reading will quickly prove to be a waste of time. *Stop.* Other books or articles will whet your appetite for more information on a subject and send you on a treasure hunt. You're in control of the quest. Often you'll find yourself longing for help in coping with some ministerial situation. That sense of "I wish I could do a better job of dealing with this" should be a primary impetus toward reading in a particular area.

Christianity Today, read by many evangelicals, and *The Christian Century*, popular among mainline Protestants, seem to play central roles as news and opinion journals. Both make an effort to deal with current areas of theological and ethical debate. The journal *Leadership* and the Alban Institute journal *Congregations* address practical aspects of ministry. I've found both to be quite helpful. For Baptists the online journal EthicsDaily.com, for which I have written, is finding a place as a meaningful commentator on current events. The evangelical Web site Crosswalk.com provides a number of helpful resources. The National Council of Churches also provides regular Web updates at councilofchurches.org. Obviously, I've made some effort here to offer resources from across the opinion spectrum, and I recommend as a growth strategy that you consider reading regularly the writings of those with whom you disagree.

In addition to general professional reading, of course, it's important also to keep up with what's going on in your denomination. The quality of denominational newspapers and journals varies widely. Still, they're often the best vehicle for discovering what's going on and who's doing it. Subscribe to your group's publication and read it. If no journal or paper for your denomination even comes to mind as you read this paragraph, that's a problem. You don't have to get involved in denominational politics to be competent. Some of the best ministers I have known stayed completely out of the denominational melee. But you do need to know what's happening.

The increasing availability of online resources offers tremendous potential for enriching ministry. In a recent article in *The Christian Century*, Beth Lewis, president and CEO of Augsburg Fortress, the Evangelical Lutheran Church in America publishing house, provided a list of six Web sites of particular interest to ministers. She cited:

- www.ot-studies.com for the Old Testament and the ancient Near East
- www.ntgateway.com for the New Testament
- www.religion-online.org for many religious and theological topics
- www2.evansville.edu/ecoleweb for church history from the early church to the Reformation
- www.pitts.emory.edu/dia/searchform.cfm for religious artistry
- www.textweek.com for ecumenical study of the Revised Common lectionary[1]

Finally, a whole range of journals and Web sites serve those who practice a particular ministry specialty or espouse a specific cause. *Sojourners* serves those who are interested in spirituality and social justice (www.sojo.net). *World Vision* helps lead the fight against hunger (www.worldvision.org). The Wayne Oates Institute at www.oates.org keeps its subscribers stimulated on subjects related to pastoral care. *Homiletics* (www.homileticsonline.com), from the mainline, and Preaching (www.preaching.com), from the evangelical perspective, provide stimulating input on the art of pulpit ministry.

Youth ministry, education ministry, music ministry, liturgics, evangelism, and worship all make use of more internet resources than you can access in a lifetime. The real difficulty is deciding which ones are worth your attention. If you're not sure where to begin or which writers to trust in your field, call or send an e-mail message to your kindly old seminary professor and ask for a recommendation.

Lifelong Learning

After reading, the second major way to build a habit of growth into your ministry is to take time on a regular basis for continuing education. My own denomination, the American Baptist Churches in the U.S.A, values continuing education so highly that it provides a space on ministers' denominational résumés to list continuing-education courses you've attended and credits you've earned. Seminaries love to provide brief intensive one- or two-week enrichment courses for ministers in practice. Many denominations and parachurch groups also provide less formal opportunities for growth through conferences on a variety of ministry-related topics.

The key factor enabling you to pursue this form of growth is to build into your contract with the congregation time and money specifically designated for continuing education. Churches will often provide a week or two a year of paid leave for the purpose of attending educational conferences or denominational meetings. Some denominations require congregations to do so. The most important thing is to have that conversation with the congregation's representatives during the negotiation of your initial contract. Congregations will usually agree in advance that they want their ministers to grow intellectually and professionally. Unfortunately, however, in congregations that are not already in the habit of supporting their minister's continuing education, the realities of church finance might make it difficult for leaders to imagine adding funds for such ventures other than at key moments such as the calling of a new minister. (The only exception to that rule I ever witnessed occurred when one congregation, in the aftermath of sexual misconduct by a senior minister, added money for its staff to take courses in clinical pastoral education on a rotating basis.)

In some cases, ministers will formalize their continuing-education ventures by seeking a further professional degree. Over the past 30 years, the doctor of ministry degree, available from a number of seminaries around the country, has been developed as a terminal degree specifically geared to pastors. The degree is intended as an opportunity for ministers in practice to continue their education in an area of specialization. Less academic and more practical than the doctor of philosophy degree, doctor of ministry programs usually include some seminar work and a formal ministry project and report pursued in the context of one's own congregation. Academic types often look down their noses at the D.Min. as insufficiently "academic," but my own observation is that the value of the degree depends specifically upon the institution offering it and the individual pursuing it.

The D.Min., of course, is by no means the only option for ministers. Degree studies in pastoral care, business administration, spiritual direction, social work, and every other academic discipline are available. The development of accredited online education makes such options more accessible than ever before. Options for broadening your credentials are limited only by your own time, money, interest, imagination, and ability.

Professional Networking

Beyond the educational and training benefits we gain from attending conferences or taking classes, some ministers will be interested in developing networking habits within their denomination or other organizations with the goal of enhancing their professional opportunities. This third habit for growth could be loosely described as learning how to climb the ladder or, more positively, contributing to the work of the wider church or serving the larger community. Some may consider such a concern profoundly unethical, as though there were something inherently unseemly about clergy expressing personal ambition. I certainly agree that Christian ministers are biblically enjoined from seeking power for its own sake and that the needs of the congregation we serve must come before outside activities. On the other hand, you have an obligation to develop and use your own abilities to their maximum, while keeping in mind your overall priorities. Fully using your talents comes under the heading of good stewardship. And sometimes, if you are to express your gifts, you need first to create the opportunity to do so.

Achieving the opportunity to use your talents fully arises in most settings from being present and participating actively in the work of the organization. If you want to help run your denomination or a parachurch group or community-based ministry someday, volunteer for a local or regional committee today. Attend meetings. Keep up with what's going on, and show your support of the organization's aims and priorities.

Personal Networking

A fourth, less formalized habit for growth consists of networking with other ministers on a regular basis. Many clergy participate in local ministerial association meetings, lectionary study groups, prayer groups, etc., which, apart from their stated agendas, provide opportunities for exchange of ideas and sharing of information as well as personal support and, for some, social connections. Ministerial retreats and denominational meetings, whatever their stated purpose, are often about precisely this kind of networking. This "hidden" agenda was for me at least perhaps the single most important reason for attending such events. Our colleague Mike, whose comments appear throughout this book, has for years attended an informal annual retreat with pastors of similar churches for the specific purpose (along with golf!) of picking each other's brains for approaches to ministerial practice. There's also an important support component here. Parish ministry can be lonely, and some of these groups become safe places where pastors can be themselves, talk about what's really going on, and have a little fun together with someone else who really knows what ministry is like.

The informal retreat mentioned here consists of eight to 12 pastors. We come prepared to discuss five to 10 books or other resources we've read during the past year, at least one churchwide event or program that worked well and one that did not, continuing-education programs or retreats we've tried and found useful, insights into what our ministry is becoming in the decade of life we happen to have in common, and resources for sermon planning and development. More informally, we discuss emerging trends in American church life, how to approach ticklish church leadership challenges, and how better to care for ourselves. MAS

Ultimately, developing the habit of growth as a minister is dependent upon your mind-set. It's essential that we never be afraid of venturing into a new area of learning. Fear as such is not a Christian emotion. We even have a proof text from the pastoral letters to drive home the point: "For God did not give us a spirit of cowardice, but rather a spirit of power and of love and of self-discipline" (2 Tim. 1:7). If, like Erica in our opening vignette, you're intimidated by a particular idea or area of innovation, try viewing that intimidation as an indication that it represents precisely the direction in which you should seek to grow. Growing as ministers involves disciplining ourselves to practice constant curiosity about how to do our work more faithfully and more effectively.

Growth beyond the Norm

The habits for growth discussed above can be cultivated by any minister in virtually any setting. Before bringing this book to a close, however, I want to advocate that you consider a few ventures that don't necessarily fall within the normal bounds of professional growth in ministry but that can nonetheless move your own growth as a minister to new and rewarding levels.

Short-term Mission

The first of these possibilities is short-term mission. Whether inside or outside the country, the benefits of participating in short-term mission projects are widely touted for youth and laypeople. Such ventures give church people a broader perspective on the world and a far more realistic picture of others' needs than they ever get from learning about missions at second hand. I believe ministers gain as much as, or more than, anyone else from these efforts. Having experienced such events myself over the years in locations as varied as the Netherlands, New York City, Oklahoma's Kickapoo Indian Reservation (yes, there really is a Kickapoo Reservation), and Colorado's San Luis Valley, I've learned much more about myself and the ministries of Christ in those settings than I could ever have learned had I not gone.

Often Christians take a relatively simplistic view of the challenges of life. We think, for example, that those in poverty could change their circumstances if they chose to do so. We fail to recognize the extreme complexity of cultural norms and social, political, and economic systems that support ways of living that appear to us not to work. Experiencing those realities firsthand gives us an appreciation for other people's circumstances that we simply cannot get any other way. It also helps us evaluate our own priorities. Sometimes we discover that those who don't have all our "advantages" are quite happy and fulfilled without them.

For those who are a bit more adventurous or whose circumstances allow for longer-term service, many denominations and mission groups provide opportunities for six months or a year or two of mission service. Teaching English as a second language has become one of the most popular ways for Christians to gain access to relationships with people in countries where mission work is not permitted. The principal by-product of such efforts for those who go is often a broader appreciation of the world and its diversity than could be gained in any other way.

Travel

Apart from missions, travel generally has a broadening effect that should not be underestimated. While travel can be expensive, and ministerial salaries tend to be modest, it's worth the effort. Evensong at Yorkminster Cathedral in England and mass at Sacre Coeur in Paris, where the Eucharist has been celebrated around the clock for over a century, changed this boy from Arkansas in ways I cannot begin to describe. How can anyone be the same after watching the sun rise over the Jordan River or worshiping with the Naga of north-eastern India?

There are ways to address the issue of affordability. The first is simply to make travel a priority. Many of us spend all our extra time and money going to see family. Family is important, and no one would suggest that we neglect such visits. But it is also possible to save for occasional trips to places where we've never been. Currently in the United States a number of credit-card companies offer airline miles at the rate of one mile for every dollar charged. In our family, we buy everything with our credit card, pay the bill in full each month to avoid interest, and accumulate miles for family adventures. As I was writing this book, the three of us were able to fly from the Midwest to New York for free.

A number of reputable travel agencies specialize in tours of the Holy Land or in retracing the journeys of Paul. These companies are always looking for ministers who are willing to host such trips, gathering a group from their city or congregation. Often those who act as hosts can travel essentially free. Ministers who make these trips often find that their preaching and teaching are enhanced by seeing firsthand the places they describe. For some, the trips become profound spiritual experiences.

Geographical Mobility

I want to make one other "geographical" suggestion that for some readers will go against the grain. As a pastor I have served in the Ohio Valley, Texas, and California. I now teach in South Dakota. While moving around the country has meant that we have seldom lived close to family, it has also added immeasurably to our appreciation for both the diversity and the unity of American culture. We have learned much about the ethnic and social mixes of various regions. We have learned to speed up in the cities and to follow agricultural rhythms with the country folk. I've run a snowblower at 5:30 a.m. and 10 degrees below zero, and I've spent my lunch hour sunning on the shore of San Francisco Bay—not, of course, on the same day! We've learned that a single denomination may carry within its communion an incredible variety of practice and perspective. We've learned that provincialism is by no means limited to the provinces. I know that many ministers want to serve as close to home as possible. Good arguments can be made for that perspective. From my point of view, however, an openness to geographical change can significantly enrich your family's experience, your own perspective on life, and your approach to ministry.

Cross-cultural Ministry

Some folks, however, just prefer to stay close to home. The good news in America these days is that geography is no barrier to an experience of diversity. The upper Midwest, where I live, is generally considered to be the least ethnically diverse area in the country. Yet our small midwestern city has significant communities of people speaking more than 30 languages. We have a Native American population almost equal in percentage to the African American population in the South. And even the smallest towns in our region are finding that significant numbers of Hispanics and Asians are moving in.

Clearly, opportunities for cross-cultural ministry abound. One church I served became heavily involved in refugee resettlement. Relating to someone from a different culture quickly forces you back to basics. You learn to communicate without words. You learn that a smile goes a long way in any language. You realize that the cast-off furniture from people's closets and attics can create what feels like a palace to someone who's been used to sleeping on dirt. You discover that not everybody in this world even knows how an American toilet works, much less how to catch a crosstown bus or to fill out an employment application. Yet they come to us with incredible cultural riches of their own. Their sense of community and hospitality, their profound gratitude for each day's provisions, their family values, and their ethnic artistry have much to teach us.

In the process of relating across cultures, you change in line with biblical values. In writing to the church at Corinth, Paul talks about his efforts to develop a universal Christian witness: "I have become all things to all people that I might by all means save some" (1 Cor. 9:22b). He sought to learn about and adapt to the cultures with which he dealt as a means of ministering more effectively. However one goes about it, a minister who stretches herself by new experiences will enhance her fitness for ministry. She will learn a great deal about both the universality and the adaptability of the gospel message.

Fun outside the Church

Finally, not everything we do has to be ministry. One of the very best ways to grow as a person is to find something you like to do and do it. Go camping or fishing or hiking. Join a softball team. Take a painting class. Read a British mystery. Research your family tree. This world God has given us is chock-full of exciting possibilities. Ministers more than anybody else ought to realize that and become experts in enjoying life.

Planning for Growth

Perhaps the greatest barrier to growing as a minister is simply failing to plan for your growth. Erica in our opening vignette knew that the increasing use of technology in worship would one day put pressure on her own approach. She could have set out much earlier to learn about its possibilities, but she didn't. She allowed her intimidation at the prospect of acquiring an unfamiliar skill to prevent her from moving forward. She chose to ignore the advent of change and to hope it would go away. Her choice cost her time, aggravation, and that intangible commodity of ministerial influence.

Many of us, when we leave seminary, are tired of school and eager for "real-life" experience. We fail to realize that learning forms an integral part of any profession. No salesperson, teacher, physician, or mechanic can continue successfully in business without staying up to date. So it is also for those of us in the ministry.

The question is, "How do you develop a comprehensive plan for personal and professional growth?" I want to suggest a fairly simple method that can be adapted to your own interests and needs.

Obtain a loose-leaf notebook and label a separate sheet of paper for
each of the chapters of this book. Begin by noting the things you do
well in each category. You might even star those elements which you
think strongly support your ministry. In the left margin of each sheet,
list the skills or concepts on which you want to work. Then add
columns with timetables, means of evaluation, and long-term goals.
For example, on the sheet for communication skills, you might want
to create a three-year plan for improving some specific skills in your
preaching and church communication. Here's a sample:

Skill	1st Year	2nd Year	3rd Year	Evaluation	Goal
Ability to Use Power Point	Online Course	Use in 6 sermons		Feedback Questionnaire	PP as Needed
Narrative Preaching		Take J-term Course Do 4 sermons		Talkback Groups	Regular Option
Improve Newsletter	Obtain Budget for Consultant	Hire Consultant, Analyze Newsletter	Implement Changes	Ongoing Feedback from Congregation	Clear, Effective Newsletter

By repeating this process with each major skill and awareness
area of your ministry, you will get a clear idea of those areas in which
you want to grow.

For many of us the real problem will be deciding which areas we
want to work on first. You may want to spend time in thought and
prayer, seeking God's guidance as you look toward next year's priorities. You may want to talk with trusted congregational leaders
and ask their advice on what skills you need to work on next. Remember Erica! Some congregations have a pastor-parish relations
committee whose job it is to help you understand the congregation's
perceptions of your work. Often the one who will be most candid
with you is your spouse. For larger or longer-term projects such as
travel or degree programs you'll want to think about time off and
financial considerations. Some projects, such as an overseas sabbatical, might take several years to plan.

The next step in the process is to take your calendar for the coming year and to pencil in when you will take a specific initiative. If your goal involves a monthly meeting with a spiritual director, for example, how will you build that meeting into your schedule? When, weekly, will you read? If you believe it's really important this year to learn how to use PowerPoint as an aid in your teaching and preaching, you will want to build into your yearly calendar both the time and the money to take a course (or at least to work your way through a tutorial). Because most online courses follow a specific schedule, taking the course will mean that you will have to adjust your other priorities during that period. If the course falls during a time when you've already scheduled a mission trip to Mexico, you may have to adjust your priorities. When you've integrated your priorities for growth into your schedule in such a way that you have a reasonable shot at getting them done, congratulate yourself. You have a plan!

The idea here is fairly simple. By developing a plan for growth that includes a timetable, specific actions, a method of evaluation, and a long-term goal, you provide yourself with a structure within which to work. Of course, if you find yourself pursuing an area of interest that's not on the list, great! This is not like the children's story in which Frog lost his list and had to sit down because finding his list wasn't on his list. The point is rather that most of us who don't *plan* won't *do*. Those of us who do plan may not do all that we plan, but the chances are that we will do *something*.

By the way, if you're one of those few who haven't yet surrendered to the computer age, it's time to give up the battle! You need to learn the basics, both for the sake of your own work and to help you understand the lives of your parishioners. Take a course.

Once a year it's a good idea to take at least a one-day retreat to review and revamp your growth plan. For those who have a high need to complete tasks, it's especially important to remember that this plan has no purpose beyond helping you think clearly toward your future. If you don't get all of this year's objectives done, there's always next year. With every passing year our interests, circumstances, ambitions, and priorities will almost certainly be modified. By revisiting our plans regularly, we give ourselves the opportunity to adjust them to the realities of life.

Planning for Long-term Goals

In addition to this kind of skills-related list, it's also helpful to think on a regular basis about your own longer-term goals for your ministry. For example, I had always known that I hoped someday to spend a portion of my career teaching in a seminary. As I approached my early 50s, I began to realize that the opportunity to make such a change from the pastorate might be beginning to slip away from me. That realization helped prompt me to give the search for a teaching opportunity one more try. That search resulted in my present position. As Christians we believe in the providence of God in our lives. With no effort whatsoever on your part, God could drop the perfect opportunity in your lap. But we also believe that God expects us to take responsibility for our own personal and professional development. You're much more likely to move forward if you take at least some initiative on your own.[2]

Sometimes, of course, we reach an impasse. We may feel discontented with where we are but not have a clear sense about whether we need to make a career change or, indeed, what kind of change might be helpful. Because both clergy and congregations often assume that parish ministry is a divine call for lifelong service, we may feel guilty for even contemplating doing something else. In reality, such periodic reevaluation is a natural and healthy part of every career, including a career in ministry. One of the wisest mentors I've ever known told me that he reviewed his calling to a particular place of service once every six months. He did so not to confuse himself but rather to make certain that he remained in the center of God's will for his life.

As I was completing my comments on this book, I went for a walk with two pastor friends and asked them what they would say about this book's basic ideas of competence in functioning as a minister. They said two things: First, a minister needs to have a heartfelt compassion for people. Without that compassion, a minister has nothing to offer. Second, to keep going, a minister needs to learn to live with ambiguity. Much of a minister's life will be spent in dealing with situations for which there is no clear outcome. JAH

A few years ago, at such a time of reevaluation in my own life, I discovered that my own denomination, in cooperation with several other communions, maintains a network of career centers scattered around the nation. The purpose of these centers is to provide clergy with testing, counseling, and evaluation to support maximum job satisfaction. Over a period of a couple of days at one of these centers, you can take a series of personality and interest inventories, have several conversations with a counselor, and receive the interpretation of your testing. The experience may simply confirm what you already knew about yourself, or it may help you put words to feelings you haven't previously been able to analyze.

If you are serving in a mainline denomination, the chances are very good that your district or regional executive can put you in touch with such a center near you. Don't worry about asking the question. Judicatory executives would much rather work with clergy who know themselves well. They'll be glad to help you find the help you need. Some judicatories see periodic career evaluation as so important that they will pay for the cost of the experience. Evangelical or less hierarchical groups may be somewhat less likely to have such a structure in place, but if that is the case for you, the chances are good that a local mental-health professional will be able to point you in the right direction. Most large cities, in addition, will have secular organizations that provide similar career evaluation services for people in the business world. While such a service may not be specifically geared to ministry, it can still be helpful in assisting you to clarify your interests. The endnote provides a link to help you locate the offices of your denomination.[3]

Assessing Your Need for Growth

Socrates is reputed to have said, "The unexamined life is not worth living." For ministers, it is not so much that the unexamined life is not worth living as it is that our lives, when unexamined, may not be all that they could become. A significant emphasis throughout this book is that competence as a minister is enhanced by taking responsibility for your life as it is and for where you want it to go. Skills can be learned. Self-awareness can grow. The more honest we are with ourselves about where we are and where we want to go, the more likely we are to grow in competence and satisfaction.

You may have noticed that most chapters of this book have ended with some suggestions for assessing whether you're accomplishing your purpose, as discussed in the chapter. As you plan to grow as a minister, the ultimate assessment of success is your own. The general question "Is your ministry moving forward?" carries within itself many specifics. Do you understand yourself better than you did five years ago? Are you handling stress well? Are your communication skills growing? Are you developing good interpersonal skills? Do you feel comfortable and effective as a leader? Are you growing in your walk with Christ? Are you feeling happier and more fulfilled in your work? If not, maybe it's time to plan to grow. Take advantage of this book and the resources it has suggested, and design your next steps in self development. If your answer to the preceding questions is "Yes!"—then well done. Chances are, you are already implementing many of the insights this book provided. If so, give thanks, and keep asking what God wants to do next with your life.

Notes

Chapter 1, From My Mother's Womb

1. Edwin H. Friedman, *Generation to Generation: Family Process in Church and Synagogue* (New York: Guilford Press, 1985).
2. Reggie McNeal, *A Work of Heart: Understanding How God Shapes Spiritual Leaders* (San Francisco: Jossey-Bass, 2000).
3. I'm thinking here of the pastoral care and counseling movement in theological studies, particularly as exemplified by Seward Hiltner and Wayne Oates.
4. Friedman, *Generation to Generation*, 195-196.
5. Ibid., 23.
6. Ibid., 208.
7. Ibid., 217.
8. McNeal, *A Work of Heart*, 117.
9. Friedman, *Generation to Generation*, 197-198.
10. G. Lloyd Rediger, *Clergy Killers: Guidance for Pastors and Congregations under Attack* (Louisville: Westminster John Knox, 1997).
11. In this context, one is reminded of the amusing and cogent little book on change titled *Who Moved My Cheese?* by Spencer Johnson (New York: G. P. Putnam's Sons, 1998). Congregations often keep running the same maze long after the cheese has gone away!
12. Friedman, *Generation to Generation*, 236-242.
13. Peter L. Steinke, *How Your Church Family Works: Understanding Congregations as Emotional Systems* (Herndon, Va.: Alban Institute, 1993), 35. Chart used by permission.

14. A. J. Hovestadt, W. T. Anderson, F. A. Piercy, S. W. Cochran, and M. Fine, "A Family-of-Origin Scale," *Journal of Marital and Family Therapy* 11, no. 3 (1985): 287–297. Used by permission of American Association for Marriage and Family Therapy.

Chapter 2, *I Press on toward the Goal*

1. Some, of course, will quarrel with the suggestion that the will to succeed should be part of a pastor's makeup. I contend that Christians should define success differently from the way others may, but also that initiative, appropriately understood, is an essential part of a minister's character. The will to succeed may relate to the will to bring our congregants further on their journey of faith, to be successful in that endeavor.
2. William Pauck, "The Ministry in the Time of the Continental Reformation," in H. Richard Niebuhr and Daniel D. Williams, eds., *The Ministry in Historical Perspectives* (New York: Harper & Row, 1983), 144.
3. George Herbert, *The Country Parson, The Temple,* ed. John N. Wall, Jr. (New York: Paulist Press, 1981), 65.
4. Herbert, *The Country Parson,* 55.
5. Ibid., 56.
6. Frederick Buechner, *The Alphabet of Grace* (San Francisco: Harper & Row, 1970), 40-41.
7. Mike Altena, Self-Assessment Paper, Readiness for Ministry Colloquium, North American Baptist Seminary (spring 2004): 2. Used by permission.
8. David Hansen, *The Art of Pastoring: Ministry Without All the Answers* (Downers Grove, Ill.: Intervarsity Press, 1994), 15.
9. David Keirsey and Marilyn Bates, *Please Understand Me: Character and Temperament Types,* 4th ed. (Del Mar, Calif.: Prometheus Nemesis Book Company, 1984).
10. M. Scott Peck, *The Road Less Traveled* (New York: Simon and Schuster, 1978), 271.

Chapter 3, *If the Trumpet Gives an Uncertain Sound*

1. Steve Clapp, *Ministerial Competency Report* (Sidell, Ill.: C-4 Publications, 1982), 51.

2. Ibid., 52.
3. Ibid., 53.
4. George Herbert, *The Country Parson, The Temple*, 56-57.
5. William Willimon, *Pastor: The Theology and Practice of Ordained Ministry* (Nashville: Abingdon, 2002), 68-69.
6. Henri Nouwen, *Creative Ministry* (New York: Doubleday Image Books, 1991), Introduction, n.p.
7. Gaylord Noyce, *Pastoral Ethics: Professional Responsibilities of the Clergy* (Nashville: Abingdon, 1988), 205.
8. Wayne Oates, *The Christian Pastor*, revised and enlarged edition (Philadelphia: Westminster, 1977), 44.
9. See, for example, Karen A. McClintock, *Preventing Sexual Abuse in Congregations: A Resource for Leaders* (Herndon, Va.: Alban Institute, 2004).
10. See my convocation address, "Preaching in a Congregational Context," *Review and Expositor*, vol. 100 (summer 2003): 375–382.
11. Thomas C. Long, *The Witness of Preaching* (Louisville: Westminster John Knox, 1989).
12. Harry Emerson Fosdick, quoted in Richard Lischer, ed., *The Company of Preachers* (Grand Rapids: Eerdmans, 2002), 395.
13. Long, *The Witness of Preaching*, 187-188.

Chapter 4, A Time to Every Purpose

1. Ronald D. Sisk, *Surviving Ministry* (Macon: Smyth & Helwys, 1997), 79-82.
2. Mike Altena, Self-Assessment Paper, 5.
3. George Barna, *Turnaround Churches* (Ventura, Calif.: Regal Books, 1993), 52.
4. Wayne Oates, "The Healthy Minister," in *The Minister's Own Mental Health* (Great Neck, N.Y.: Channel Press, 1961), 16.
5. Roy M. Oswald, *Clergy Self-Care: Finding a Balance for Effective Ministry* (Herndon, Va.: Alban Institute, 1991), 125-127.
6. Kenneth Blanchard and Spencer Johnson, *The One Minute Manager* (New York: Berkley Books, 1981).
7. David S. Belasic and Paul M. Schmidt, *The Penguin Principles: A Survival Guide for Clergy Seeking Maturity in Ministry* (Lima, Ohio: CSS Publishing, 1986), 52-60.

Chapter 5, My Yoke Is Easy

1. Wayne E. Oates, *Managing Your Stress* (Philadelphia: Fortress, 1985), 9.
2. Adapted by Roy Oswald from the Holmes/Rahe Life Changes Rating Scale. Published in Roy M. Oswald, "Life Changes for Clergy," in *Clergy Self-Care: Finding a Balance for Effective Ministry* (Herndon, Va.: Alban Institute, 1991), 29–31. Used by permission.
3. See "Rest: The Gift of God in Christ," in Wayne E. Oates, *Your Right to Rest* (Philadelphia: Westminster, 1984), 92-97.
4. Joseph Phelps, *More Light, Less Heat: How Dialogue Can Transform Christian Conflicts into Growth* (San Francisco: Jossey-Bass, 1999).
5. Carolyn Schrock-Shenk and Lawrence Ressler, eds., *Making Peace with Conflict: Practical Skills for Conflict Transformation* (Scottsdale, Pa.: Herald Press, 1999).
6. See Glen H. Stassen, *Just Peacemaking: Transforming Initiatives for Justice and Peace* (Louisville: Westminster John Knox, 1992).

Chapter 6, Blessed Are the Peacemakers

1. John Savage, *Listening and Caring Skills: A Guide for Groups and Leaders* (Nashville: Abingdon, 1996).
2. Ibid., 16.
3. Ibid., 23.
4. Ibid., 39-48.
5. Wayne E. Oates, *The Christian Pastor* (Philadelphia: Westminster 1964), 158ff. (This work is also available in a third edition, published in 1982.)
6. David S. Belasic and Paul M. Schmidt, *The Penguin Principles: A Survival Guide for Clergy Seeking Maturity in Ministry* (Lima, Ohio: CSS Publishing Co., 1986), 52-60.
7. John Galloway, Jr., *Ministry Loves Company: A Survival Guide for Pastors* (Louisville: Westminster John Knox, 2003), 9ff.
8. Jim Herrington, Mike Bonem, and James H. Furr, *Leading Congregational Change: A Practical Guide for the Transformational Journey* (San Francisco: Jossey-Bass, 2000).

9. Andrew D. Lester, *The Angry Christian: A Theology for Care and Counseling* (Louisville: Westminster John Knox, 2003).

Chapter 7, I Saw the Holy City

1. See "The Leadership Situation Facing American Congregations," Alban Institute (September 2001).
2. Jeremy Wiersema, Self-Assessment Paper, Pastoral Ministry 301, North American Baptist Seminary (spring 2004). Used by permission.
3. See, for example, J. Robert Clinton, *Leadership Emergence Theory* (Altadena, Calif.: Barnabas Publishers, 1989).
4. Jim Herrington, Mike Bonem, and James H. Furr, *Leading Congregational Change: A Practical Guide for the Transformational Journey* (San Francisco: Jossey-Bass, 2000).
5. Ibid., *Leading Congregational Change*, 53ff.
6. Bill Thrall, Bruce McNicol, and Ken McElrath, *The Ascent of a Leader: How Ordinary Relationships Develop Extraordinary Character and Influence* (San Francisco: Jossey-Bass, 1999).
7. I learned this concept from my own Christian ethics professor, the late Dr. Henlee H. Barnette. He offers this definition of the Greek meaning of *agape* in contrast to the exaggerated emotionalism that is often mistaken for love in contemporary Christian contexts.

Chapter 8, Abide in Me

1. Name withheld, "Readiness for Ministry Self-Assessment," North American Baptist Seminary (spring 2004).
2. Richard J. Foster, *Celebration of Discipline: The Path to Spiritual Growth* (San Francisco: Harper & Row, 1978), and *Prayer: Finding the Heart's True Home* (San Francisco: HarperSanFrancisco, 1992).
3. Foster, *Prayer*, 6.
4. Marcus J. Borg. *Reading the Bible Again for the First Time* (San Francisco: HarperSanFrancisco, 2001).
5. Jane E. Vennard, *A Praying Congregation: The Art of Teaching Spiritual Practice* (Herndon, Va.: Alban Institute, 2005).

6. Jeannette A. Bakke. *Holy Invitations: Exploring Spiritual Direction.* (Grand Rapids: Baker Books, 2000); Keith R. Anderson and Randy Reese, *Spiritual Mentoring: A Guide for Seeking and Giving Direction* (Downers Grove, Ill.: Intervarsity Press, 1999).

7. Thomas G. Long, *Testimony: Talking Ourselves into Being Christian* (San Francisco: Jossey-Bass, 2004).

8. William H. Willimon, *Pastor: The Theology and Practice of Ordained Ministry* (Nashville: Abingdon, 2002, 229-230).

9. Ronald D. Sisk, *Surviving Ministry* (Macon, Ga.: Smyth & Helwys Publishing, 1997).

10. Richard J. Foster. *Money, Sex and Power: The Challenge of the Disciplined Life* (San Francisco: Harper & Row, 1985).

11. Ibid., 71-73.

12. Gaylord Noyce, *Pastoral Ethics: Professional Responsibilities of the Clergy* (Nashville: Abingdon, 1988).

13. Ibid., 130.

14. Ed, for example, might well benefit from some of the classics of Christian devotion, such as John of the Cross's *Dark Night of the Soul* or John Bunyan's *Pilgrim's Progress*.

Chapter 9, House on the Rock

1. "Web sites for Bible and theology research," Beth Lewis, *The Christian Century* 122, no. 4 (February 22, 2005): 45.

2. The following books from Alban might be helpful as you plan: Jill M. Hudson, *When Better Isn't Enough: Evaluation Tools for the 21st-Century Church*; Rochelle Melander and Harold Eppley, *The Spiritual Leader's Guide to Self-Care*; and A. Richard Bullock and Richard J. Bruesehoff, *Clergy Renewal: The Alban Guide to Sabbatical Planning.*

3. The Hartford Institute for Religious Research maintains a Web site that lists contact information on U.S. denominations and religious groups. Log on to http://hartsem.edu/org/faith_denominations_homepages.html.